FUN IN

ACAPULCO

1988

Susan Wagner

Published by
FODOR'S TRAVEL PUBLICATIONS, INC.
New York & London

ISBN 0–679–01504–3
ISBN 0–340–42266–1 (Hodder & Stoughton)

Maps and plans by Burmar
Illustrations by Ted Burwell

New titles in the series

Barbados
Jamaica

also available

Bahamas
Disney World and the Orlando Area
Las Vegas
London
Maui
Montreal
New Orleans
New York City
Paris
Rio
San Francisco
St. Martin/Sint Maarten
Waikiki

MANUFACTURED IN THE UNITED STATES OF AMERICA
10 9 8 7 6 5 4 3 2 1

Contents

Maps and plans

Introduction

Acapulco is the ultimate seaside resort. The unexpected is the rule, not the exception, and is guaranteed to happen if you let it. A school teacher finds herself dancing on the table. A bus driver treats everyone in the house to drinks. A baroness goes to an all-night coffeeshop in a ballgown and diamonds—and this is only the beginning.

It all begins as the car curves around the Scenic Highway from the airport and the beautiful bay reveals itself. No matter how many times you've arrived in Acapulco, the first breathtaking view of the bay never fails to give you goosebumps.

Most resorts this pretty have a passive attitude. They provide some natural beauty and perhaps an infrastructure of hotels, restaurants, discos, and so forth, but visitors are left on their own from there on.

Not so in Acapulco—they take things a step further. It seems that every one of the over one million people who live here is revved up and ready to help you have a good time. The animate and the inanimate combine to make for an unbeatable combination.

Acapulco has one of the most beautiful bays and

some of the best weather in the world. There are approximately 360 days of sunshine to enjoy every year. Balmy tropical temperatures seldom fall below 80 degrees. The water is always close to a comfortable body temperature, and beaches are a dream come true—they look just like the ones you see on travel posters but hardly ever find.

Hotels are big and spacious. Leading deluxe and five-star establishments are spread over greater pieces of property, have larger rooms and more opulent public areas than most hotels of similar classifications in other parts of the world. This is where most resorts stop and where Acapulco keeps going. They want to make sure that your times will be good.

Just about every water sport known to man can be practiced here. Discos dazzle as they do in no other part of the world. Restaurants are a special part of the tongue-in-cheek fun, too. The service as well as the food and the view make meals memorable.

Very few things are hidden away. Most major hotels, shops, discos, and restaurants are located along seven miles of the seaside highway, Costera Miguel Aleman, which has been nicknamed "The Strip."

One of the greatest things about Acapulco is that there's plenty of Mexican flavor, too. In many ways, life goes on as it has for centuries even though the city is also a jet-set resort. Fishermen leave at dawn with giant nets, cooks prepare ancient recipes, workers mold clay and paint pottery as their ancestors have for centuries. The wide-open municipal market is as colorful and as varied and as vital to everyday life as any other in the country. On Sundays, families take a walk or listen to a band concert in the Zocalo (main square) as they did in days gone by. This sophisticated international playground is as Mexican as they come.

The fact that there are no daily schedules to follow is another great asset. This is a place that also lets you dress as you like and do as you like. Anything goes, as long as it's not against the law. It's hard to find a resort as permissive as Acapulco.

There are few "rules" to spoil the fun. Go barefoot to a disco, wear an evening dress with a wet ponytail and a flower in your hair, stay in your bathing suit until well after midnight, sneak away to have a short siesta under a palm tree—and no one will even blink an eyelash.

Everything from sophisticated to primitive entertainment can be found: the long, unspoiled beaches of Pie de la Cuesta and Revolcadero, the primitive Coyuca Lagoon nature preserve, the bustling central area which is the tropical "downtown" for the 1.8 million permanent inhabitants (Acapulco is one of Mexico's largest cities), the town beaches where people gather in early morning and late afternoon to watch the fishermen come and go, the sophisticated "Strip" of glittering hotels, restaurants, shops, and discos, and "Old Acapulco" where the fun began over a quarter of a century ago. It's all yours to take as you please at your own pace. Every day can be different. You only have to plan it and select what suits your mood.

There are a few things that take a bit of getting used to, though. At 3:30 A.M., someone might ask if you want to go to another disco "since it's still early." If you're invited to dinner in a private home at 10 P.M., only the servants actually arrive at 10. Most evenings begin late, so take a candy bar along to keep your stomach from growling until a meal is served.

Nahuatl Indians gave Acapulco its name, which means "Place of the Reeds." Today, there's not a reed in sight, but there are plenty of other things to see. The Spaniards discovered Acapulco, made it into an important port for their trade with the Orient, and built Fort San Diego to protect it.

The tourist boom began about 40 years ago, and since then the place hasn't stopped growing. The tropical natural beauty and freewheeling lifestyle made it a success from the very first minute.

Acapulco's appeal is universal. Teddy Stauffer, a forward-looking Swiss who came and stayed, founded some of the things that catapulted Acapulco into international stardom. The daring divers at La Quebrada, the "Boom Boom Room," Acapulco's first dance hall, and Tequila A Go Go, its first discotheque, were all his inventions.

Anyone who thinks that Acapulco has peaked and that the excitement couldn't possibly continue should take a look at the magnificent home that the Baron and

Baroness di Portanova have built, or should take note of the results of the multimillion-dollar city-wide improvement program that was completed recently. Streets and sidewalks along The Strip were made heat absorbent, so that you can walk the seven-mile stretch in your bare feet on a hot sunny day. Electrical and telephone wires were hidden. Waters of the bay were cleaned, and non-stop programs to keep them that way have been undertaken. CiCi and Papagayo Parks, both on prime real estate along the Costera Aleman, were built for the enjoyment of all.

A construction boom was temporarily halted when the peso underwent several devaluations, but it picked up again and new facilities and *Centros Commerciales* (the Mexican term for shopping mall) are springing up all over town.

The devaluations made Acapulco even more attractive to American and Canadian visitors. In a period of a few years, exchange rates soared from 12 to over 1,000 pesos to the U.S. dollar, making Mexico one of the biggest travel bargains anywhere.

However, the economic situation has also caused more than a bit of confusion. Long-range planning is virtually impossible. Hotel rates, admission charges, restaurant prices and hours seem to be different every day. Finding out what something may cost six months from now or even tomorrow, what place will be open, or what new show or disco will be instituted—all the things that are based on a bottom line—has become about as easy as finding the code to the Rosetta Stone.

All prices mentioned here should therefore be considered as guidelines only. At this writing, the peso is hovering around 1,026 to the dollar. Planning what you want to do and how much you might spend may be more difficult than ever before, but it hasn't affected the fun one bit. Prices are still more than reasonable across the board, and crowds are coming in record-breaking numbers.

As a result of the economic situation, more Mexicans are coming to Acapulco, too, instead of travelling abroad. You can be sure that it will be overflowing on any long weekend in Mexico City and during the long Christmas and Easter school vacations.

This makes planning your next visit well ahead of time essential. When in the past you might have been able to zip down for a weekend or breeze into a restaurant on the spur of the moment, you now have to reserve well in advance.

Thankfully, the increasing popularity hasn't changed Acapulco's tropical pace and attitudes. Acapulco still forces you to gear down and relax. Get used to it. Almost all administrative matters from purchases to car and boat rentals take three to four times longer to complete than they would at home. Once you get into the tropical swing, you won't mind waiting. Smile, take it easy and forget about anything being completed right this minute or even overnight. Silhouettes of palm trees, spectacular sunsets, moonlight shimmering over the graceful bay, romantic restaurants, sparkling discos, and dazzling beaches will seduce you and make you forget that you were ever in a hurry.

Most business comes to a halt at lunch time, one to four P.M., so you might as well, too. Those who don't work might lunch from three to six, take a siesta from six to nine or ten, and then get revved up and ready for a night on the town. It's almost like making two days out of one. Night is when Acapulco really struts her stuff as reigning Queen of Mexican resorts. You shouldn't miss it.

General Information

Wonderful weather is Acapulco's trump card. Balmy tropical temperatures prevail year round. Acapulco is one of the few places in the world that can guarantee good weather. Odds are almost 100 to one in your favor that the sun will be out for most of the day.

The average year-round temperature is 80° F, and temperatures rarely fall below 70°. Residents call it cold when they have to wear cotton shirts with long sleeves.

The water always seems to be at a comfortable body temperature, so you never get a shock when you go in for a dip.

Most of the heavy rains fall between August and October but most showers are short. Some travelers—especially photographers—prefer the rainy season, when flowers and foliage are at the peak of their beauty and Acapulco is decked out in vivid green finery.

The only things that vary in this tropical paradise are the humidity and the crowds. December 15 to Easter, "The Season," are the driest months, and your odds of having bright sunshine from dawn to dusk couldn't be better. Of course, you'll get hot on the beach or in the discos, but the heat is dryer than it is during the rest of the year.

The humidity escalates gradually from July to October, but if you don't mind it you can save as much as 40 percent on hotel rates. The same restaurants, discos, and other facilities are still open and running. The only time that you might find a few of them closed for a week or two is in late August or early September, when some remodel and all are gearing up for the season.

Those who like good weather without the crowds, and those who want to get an early start on their tans, come in June or between November 15 and December 15.

Everybody likes The Season. Jet setters, home owners, and die-hard revelers come then, when the town is most crowded. Crowds get smaller between January 1 and Easter, when Mexican children have to be in school, except for Washington's birthday. August is another Mexican family vacation month, but crowds clear out after Labor Day. Group package tours, charters, and special fares are usually prevalent in the summer months and early fall, when hoteliers want to beef up business, but now that the word about reasonable prices is out, Acapulco is enjoying ever-greater popularity, and has turned into a sellers' market. So *plan ahead to avoid disappointment.*

WHAT TO WEAR

One of the greatest things about Acapulco dressing is that anything, and we mean *anything,* goes. If it's outrageous and tropical, put it on and you'll be glad you did. Everything about Acapulco dressing customs defies world norms—as well as the expected. You'll see people wearing bathing suits at midnight and long gauzy dresses during the day. This is the place where you can leave your dressing inhibitions at home and let your imagination run wild.

Your neckline can touch your ears or your navel. Some attempt should be made to cover the parts of your body that should be covered, but if the attempts are weak, most people will overlook it.

Getting dressed for an evening out is unabashed pleasure. You can be provocative or prim, crazy or conservative. You can follow your favorite fantasy, invent a costume, put it on and no one will bat an eye. You can put a shirt over your bathing suit or don diamonds and a ball gown and fit right in. This is one of the few places in the world where a woman who wears either may just slick back fresh-from-the-pool or ocean-wet hair and plop a flower behind her ear. You can leave hair spray (it gets gummy in the tropics) and elaborate coiffures at home along with fussy cocktail dresses and winter clothes.

Men have it even better. A fresh shirt and slacks are just about as formal as you'll need to get. A light blazer or tropical-weight jacket is a good idea for air-conditioned places, but all socks and ties can be left behind.

However, no matter what you wear, you'll want to look neat and well put together, since everyone else who dines in the most popular restaurants and dances in the most dazzling discos will be well decked out.

NOT TO FORGET

Though Acapulco is chockablock with sundries, you won't want to waste valuable sun or fun time searching for a specific item that you forgot. Take time to double check that the following things are in your suitcase:

• Women should bring all of your favorite *cosmetics*, including shampoo and nail polish. Your brand may be here, but your shade may not. Bring two lipsticks in case one melts.

• A small *calculator*. You'll be better at bargaining if you can figure out the price on the spot.

● *Toothpaste.* Often there is a serious shortage, so bring more than you need. There are also periodical shortages of aspirin, Anacin, etc. Excedrin doesn't seem to exist in Mexico. Stock up before you leave.

● Plenty of your favorite *suntan lotion and screens.* The sun is strong. Name U.S. brands cost more and not all are available. The same goes for *film.*

● Extra *batteries* for clocks, watches, and cameras. They're as easy to find as needles in a haystack.

● An extra collapsible *suitcase* or duffel bag. This is not only for souvenirs. It may keep you out of an expensive jam if a suitcase breaks. Good Mexican luggage is expensive. So is bad Mexican luggage.

● Sexy beach and evening *sandals.* Forget about finding any decent shoe if you wear a narrow width in any size over seven, or if you're looking for flats; Mexican women like their heels three inches high or more.

● *Sneakers.* They're there, but hard to find.

● *Dental floss.* Mexican dental floss is terrible.

● *Sunglasses.* The price is usually double what it is at home, and the selection is limited.

● A collapsible *umbrella,* if you travel during May through October.

● A sturdy *change purse.* Many Mexican coins are large and heavy! Normal wallet change purses cannot accommodate them.

TIME

Acapulco is on Central Standard Time year round, so it's one hour behind (earlier than) New York (except for Daylight Saving Time, when it's two), the same time as Chicago (one hour earlier than Chicago when the U.S. is on Daylight Savings Time), one hour ahead of Denver (the same time as Denver during U.S. Daylight Time), and two hours ahead of (later than) California except during Daylight Time, when it is only one hour ahead of (later than) California.

ENTRY

North Americans need a passport, birth certificate, or military identification card to obtain a free Tourist Card. It's available from travel agents, airlines (the airline check-in personnel at points of departure will usually ask for it and stamp it), Mexican consulates, or at entry points.

Fill it out carefully and sign in the *two* places that specify signature. This will expedite your time at the Immigration desk. One copy will be collected at Immigration upon arrival. The second will be collected at Immigration upon departure. *Don't lose track of that second copy.* You can't leave the country without that important bit of paper. The process of replacing it can be complicated and take up valuable sun and sightseeing time. So make sure that you put your card in a safe place.

Contact the U.S. Consular Representative or the Secretaria de Turismo immediately if you lose your copy of the Tourist Card. The U.S. Consular representative has an office in the Club del Sol Hotel near Big Boy on the corner of the Costera and Los Reyes Catolicos. Office hours are from 10:00 A.M. to 1:00 P.M. weekdays. The telephone number is 5–66–00. The Secretaria de Turismo is across from CiCi.

Canadians need passports and Tourist Cards.

ARRIVAL

Arrivals are Acapulco's fatal flaw. There is no easy way to get into this beautiful port—as the airport and airport transportation are handled by local authorities under Federal Jurisdiction.

As soon as you step off the plane you must begin operating under the premise that anything this good is worth waiting for and worth fighting for.

Immigration. Flights that stop in Mexico City occasionally require that passengers pass through Immigration there. Planes usually have landing slots at an extreme end of the terminal, which is inevitably the opposite end from Immigration. It's a *long* walk, and you should stick close to the airline representative who is your leader; he's your only contact with your ongoing flight and this is a *big* airport. To make things worse, passengers usually have to take all personal belongings off the aircraft, even if you reboard the same plane. Be sure to have your passport, Tourist Card, and other documents handy.

Upon landing in Acapulco, buses carry you from the plane to the terminal. You might have to stand on the runway getting hot under more than the collar until the buses arrive, so dress in layers if you're arriving from a cold climate.

Once in the terminal, get out your patience because:

- You'll have to guess which carousel has your luggage. Flight numbers are not posted.
- Immigration has a perpetually skeleton crew of two to four agents to handle several flights and several hundred people who arrive at the same time.
- You usually have to get your baggage from the carousel to Customs by yourself. The distance isn't far but it is if your luggage is heavy.
- Customs is usually easy if you're not carrying anything illegal, but don't leave your copy of *Playboy* or *Hustler* in plain view unless you want to say Adios to it.
- Once you pass Customs there are friendly porters to help. A big smile goes a long way. Porters are tipped about 500–1,000 pesos per bag. Having pesos on hand is a big help. About $15–$20 U.S. worth will get you from Immigration to your hotel.

Getting from the airport to your hotel. Just when you think your troubles are over, they begin again! Private taxis are not permitted to carry passengers from the airport to town. Getting transportation from the airport is total chaos. The system is complicated and understaffed. So, leave a friend with your luggage and jump right into the fray.

- Look for the name of your hotel and the number of its

zone on the overhead sign on the walkway out in front of the building.

- Elbow your way in to the two-person desk for your *Zona.*

You'll discover that you have a choice of the following (Rates quoted are to Zone 2, which is about the center of "The Strip."):

- Bus (Greyhound size). It costs approximately $1.70 U.S. per person.
- Combi. It accommodates seven people at about $2.80 U.S. per person.
- If you're lucky and can find one, you can hire a sedan for $15–$20. There is a small booth at the end of the car-rental desks outside on the extreme north end of the terminal. They sometimes also have limosines, which cost $25–$30—depending on your destination —when you can find them.

Especially if it's your first visit, limousines or sedans are advisable. Unfortunately, they are unavailable more often than not. Our advice: pay anything you must to get private transportation. All other methods involve long waits and crowded conditions.

Regardless of how you travel, buy *one way only* and plan to take a taxi back to the airport. When you leave your hotel and Acapulco the above alternatives require that you be ready too far in advance and you'll probably end up losing valuable sun time while you wait for them to arrive. Any taxi is allowed to go from town *to* the airport. Average taxi fare from The Strip to the airport is about $6–$8.

Once you've checked into your hotel, you can relax. *Then* the fabulous Acapulco fun begins.

DEPARTURE

Departure is much easier than arrival, but here are a few hints:

- Taxi to the airport at least one and a half or two hours early for international flights, one hour for domestic flights. On weekends in season make it two hours *for sure!* And earlier if your plane stops in Mexico City. Flights between Acapulco and Mexico City are crowded all year round, but the check-in is more chaotic in season.

- Make sure you have your copy of your Tourist Card. They'll collect it at Immigration when you leave.
- The Departure Tax is $10 U.S. for international flights and about $2.60 U.S. for domestic flights. Sometimes, domestic taxes are included in the price of your ticket. If not, they can be paid in pesos or dollars. You pay the tax and get your boarding card stamped before going through security.
- Last-minute gifts can be purchased at the airport *before* you pass Immigration. There is a bar, restaurant, and bank in that area, too. Once you have passed Immigration there's little to buy, eat, or do.
- If you want to change pesos back to dollars, there's an Exchange House *(Cambio)* at Gate C.

AIRLINE NUMBERS

It is best to make reservations before you leave the U.S. and stick to them. Mexican computers seem to break down all the time, and waits in the ticket offices for the two international Mexican carriers (Aeromexico and Mexicana) are always long. Though the Mexican carriers both have offices at two locations, some carriers only have offices at the airport. You can waste a lot of time if you try to do anything but reconfirm reservations.

Aeromexico offices are located at Costera, No. 286, about one quarter of the way down the Costera between Papagayo Park and the Zocalo. The other location is on the second floor above V.I.P.'s in the Torre de Acapulco. Mexicana de Aviacion is in Hotel las Hamacas, (midway between Papagayo and the Zocalo) and in Torre de Acapulco above V.I.P.'s. American Airlines is in the Hotel Condesa del Mar. Western/Delta and Continental are at the airport. Pan Am has applied for rights to fly to Acapulco, but they have not been granted yet.

Aeromexico	5–16–25
American	4–12–44
Continental	4–69–00
Delta	4–07–16 or 4–07–97
Mexicana de Aviacion	4–68–90

MONEY MATTERS

Banks and exchange houses (*Cambios*) are the best places to change large amounts of money. Hotels take a bite in commissions.

Banking hours are 9:00 A.M.– 1:30 P.M., Monday through Friday. Banks give the best rates, but be prepared to spend a lot of time waiting in line. Usually the sole Foreign Exchange line is shared by local store owners who can take 15–30 minutes making deposits in multiple currencies. Furthermore, foreign currencies can often be exchanged only between 10:00 and 11:30 A.M.

Cambios are usually open on Saturdays and have later hours. You can "shop" for the best exchange rate if you use cambios. Some post their rates on sidewalk blackboards.. Some stores offer to change dollars, but make sure you get a good rate.

Confusing both large and small denominations is easy, so be careful. Both old and new coins and bills are in circulation. New 20-peso coins are easily mistaken for old fives or ones. The new 20- and 50-peso coins are also easy to confuse. Bills come in 10, 20, 50, 100, 500, 1,000, 2,000, 5,000, 10,000, and 20,000 denominations.

Check denominations carefully, especially at night, and be sure to have a lot of coins (100 pesos and up) and smaller bills (500s and up) for taxis.

Twenty centavos or one new peso are the coins you should never be without. It's the cost of a local call on most phones.

A 15 percent Value Added Tax (VAT) is applied to

most purchases, including food, drinks, and clothing. It is usually included in the price.

TIPPING

Tip 10–15 percent in restaurants or bars, 20 percent if the service has been excellent, but check to see if a service charge has been added before doing so. If it has, and if service has been good, a small extra tip is appropriate. Taxi drivers don't expect tips but Mexicans usually leave small change.

Gas station and parking attendants (even those at metered places downtown) and ushers expect small tips (300–500 pesos). Chambermaids should be tipped at least 1,000 pesos a day and at least 4,000–5,000 pesos for a one-week stay.

OTHER ADVICE

Avoid driving out of town at night. Slow down on curving hillside highways—they don't have guard rails. Out of town, highways are not fenced; animals roam free, and they're a menace.

● Don't pass a gas station if your tank is half full. They're few and far between.

● Most five-star hotels have rooms with a view of the ocean. Many have rooms with the *sound* of the ocean as well. If you don't like to listen to waves 24 hours a day, ask for a room on the north (mountain) side of the hotel or on the east or south sides.

● Be careful on the beach. *Never* swim when the red flags are out and remember that undertows are usually stronger in the afternoon. Don't take too much sun during the first few days. Tropical sun is strong, so take it in short doses and load up with lotions.

● If you want to call anyone above middle management, don't call until after 10:00 A.M. If you're making a social call to a Mexican, call no earlier than noon unless you're sure that your party is an early riser.

● This is something even Acapulco residents would pay to know: the best place for emergency zipper repairs on suitcases is a small open shoemaker's store, La Candela, on Ruiz Cortines St. in front of El Eco and Acesorios Ocampo. Have the taxi wait and pantomime your way through. The price is right and they do it overnight.

● If you want a receipt for a meal paid in cash, ask for a "Nota de Consumo" and have them add on the tip.

● If you are going to the Acapulco Convention Center, ask the taxi driver to take you to the Centro de Convenciones or to Acapulco Centro. Otherwise, he might take you downtown. The same goes for the Acapulco Plaza Hotel. Ask for it by name. If you just say Plaza you'll be taken to the Exelaris Hyatt Regency, which *used* to be called the Plaza. Also, don't ask to be taken just to the "market." Specify between Mercado Municipal and the Mercado de Artesanias farther downtown.

● The cylindrical "Information Booths" along the Costera will give you some information, but their major job is to sell condominiums or time sharing. They belong to a real-estate operation.

● The State of Guerrero Department of Tourism will help you find your way around and answer questions. The office is at No. 54 Costera Aleman, across from CiCi. Their information numbers are 4–10–14 and 4–63–04. They are open Monday through Saturday from 9:00 A.M. to 2:00 P.M. and from 5:00 P.M. to 7:00 P.M., and on Sundays from 9:00 A.M. to 2:00 P.M. The number to call in case of emergency is 4–61–34 or 4–61–36. It answers at the same hours. You can also get information from the Federal Department of Tourism across from Super Super. It is open 8:00 A.M.–3:30 P.M. weekdays, 10:00 A.M. –2:00 P.M. Saturdays, closed Sundays. They sometimes have maps. Tel: 5–10–41 or 5–13–04.

● Tourist police wear sky-blue short-sleeved shirts and white trousers. They patrol the tourist area, Puerto Marques, La Barra de Coyuca, and Pie de la Cuesta, to answer questions and help tourists. Their badges indicate the language they speak.

- A good rule of thumb is to be as cautious as you are at home. Keep valuables out of sight in your room.
- When parking downtown or on the Costera, lock anything that you're fond of in the trunk. If you're in a jeep, don't trust the glove compartment. Take whatever you were going to put there with you.
- Most hotels have complimentary safe-deposit boxes. Use them if you want to be extra sure.
- Don't take valuables to the beach, and don't walk the beaches at twilight or at night.
- Good news! You can use all of your appliances in Acapulco. The current is the same as it is at home—110 volts. The electricity does go off every once in a while, so bring a small flashlight. However, everything works almost all of the time.
- Some travelers like to bring or buy their own 100-watt light bulbs. Everything in Mexico seems to be under-illuminated.

YOUR STOMACH

Overdoing sun, underdoing sleep, and changing dining schedules can turn the strongest tummy into a delicate one.

To avoid stomach upsets, eat less than usual for the first three days of your trip to allow your system to become accustomed to tropical temperatures and new flavors.

Most four- and five-star hotels have their own water-purification plants now, so you can enjoy drinks with ice or brush your teeth with tap water.

If your tummy is delicate at home, ask your doctor for a prescription before you leave and take preventive doses of Pepto Bismol three times a day. If you should become ill, Streptomagna and Lomotil are available over the counter.

If none of these remedies works within 12–18 hours, your hotel, the Secretaria de Turismo, or SEME (Servicios Medicos Turisticos, Tel: 4–32–60) in the

Copacabana Hotel, which operates around the clock, can find an English-speaking doctor, but "house calls" are expensive, usually about $50 U.S.

GETTING AROUND

Getting around Acapulco is a breeze. If you stay on The Strip, you can walk almost anywhere. First-timers should cross at crosswalks, at one of the few traffic lights, or join a gaggle of strangers until you get accustomed to darting across the streets.

Taxis are plentiful, inexpensive, and easy to find along the Costera. Regular cabs display a "Libre" sign and cruise. "Sitio" cabs are radio equipped and charge slightly more. Cabs stationed by major hotels are sometimes not metered and charge more, too (usually about 200 pesos). Be alert when you enter any taxi, and discuss the fare in advance. Prices for the same trip may vary in direct relation to how much the driver likes you, but the difference is usually no more than 100 to 200 pesos (just over 50¢ U.S.).

Acapulco taxi drivers are far better than New York taxi drivers when it comes to finding places and to charging. Most taxis are blue-and-white sedans or Volkswagens, and you can sit in front. Getting a taxi out on the Costera instead of at the front door of your hotel is usually a better deal. They don't have meters; charges are by zone. Rates between principal points are usually posted in your hotel, but ask the driver before you get in, just to make sure. Also be sure to carry small change (100 peso coins and 500 bills), as drivers often claim not to have enough. From the Princess to The Strip, for example, costs about $4; from The Strip to the Zocalo is $1.50; from The Strip to Caleta is $2.50.

Rates are 500–700 pesos higher at night. No tip is expected but Mexicans usually leave small change.

At about $8.00 U.S. per hour, you can afford to have a taxi wait if you're going shopping—a luxury by U.S. standards.

NATIONAL HOLIDAYS

Banks and stores are usually closed on these dates:

January 1	New Year's Day (Año Nuevo)
February 5	Constitution Day (Dia de La Constitucion)
March 21	Benito Juarez Birthday (Natalicio de Presidente Benito Juarez)
March 31, April 1	Holy Thursday and Good Friday (Jueves Santo, and Viernes Santo)
May 1	Labor Day (Dia del Trabajo)
May 5	Puebla Day (Dia de Puebla)
September 1	President's Address (Dia del Informe)
September 16	Independence Day (Dia de la Independencia)
October 12	Columbus Day (Dia de la Raza)
November 1	Day of the Dead (Dia de los Muertos)
November 10	Mexican Revolution Day (Dia de la Revolucion Mexicana)
December 12	Virgin of Guadalupe Day (Dia de Nuestra Senora de Guadalupe)
December 25	Christmas (Navidad)
December 31	New Year's Eve (Año Nuevo)

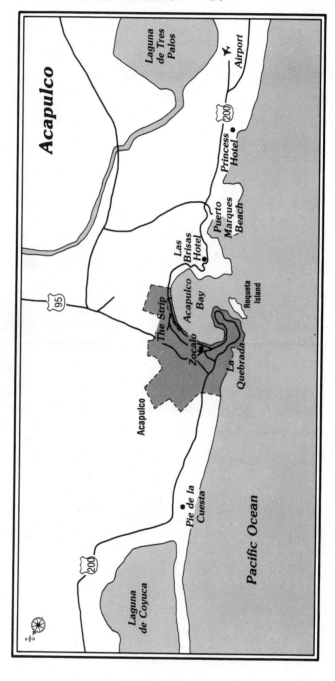

Your hotel can arrange a guide-driver for sightseeing. The rate is about $60–$70 U.S. dollars per day.

Buses run along the Costera from Caleta to Puerto Marques all day long. It's easy to pick out the brown metal stops. From the Hyatt to the end of The Strip costs about 85 pesos. Their sign says "La Base," which means the Naval Base beside the Exelaris Hyatt Regency.

Buses also go downtown to the Zocalo (main square) from The Strip, but the route does not follow the Costera for the whole way. Those marked "Hornos" take the scenic seaside route.

RENTING A VEHICLE

This is the expensive way to go, but it's the only way for those who demand instant mobility. Air-conditioned cars with automatic transmissions rent for about $60–$70 U.S. a day. Parking along the Costera is no dream either.

Avis (tel. 4–16–33), Budget (tel. 4–82–00), Dollar (tel. 4–03–66), Hertz (tel. 5–89–47), National (tel. 5–59–14), and others are here, but there's a shortage of air-conditioned cars, especially in high seasons. Be sure to specify air conditioning and automatic transmission when making your reservation if you want these extras. Include your arrival time, insist on written confirmation of your reservation, and then hope for the best. Most rental places seem to ignore reservations and rent on a first come-first served basis, regardless. If your reservation is lost and things get grim, keep your cool. Letting your temper out guarantees that you'll *never* get a car. This is a seller's market, especially at the airport. It has been our experience that Hertz personnel are more pleasant, but Avis reservations are more reliable. If you have a reservation and there are no cars, ask the counter person if he or she knows who has cars. They usually do.

Jeeps are cheaper, breezier, and more fun, but you have to know how to drive a manual shift. This is crucial, especially on Acapulco's steep hills. The only other major disadvantages are coping with coiffures and narrow skirts and not being able to lock up anything you don't want to lose. Good blue-and-white jeeps can be rented at Fast, across from the Hyatt Continental. They have more jeeps than any other company. Tels. 4–83–44 and 4-48-44. Rates are $45 U.S. a day. The price includes insurance and mileage, but gas is extra.

When registering for any car, sign for the insurance, as U.S. liability does not apply in Mexico.

The only place in town to rent motor scooters is in the lobby of the Hotel Fiesta Tortuga. They cost about $12.00 a day with gas, plus tax.

Horse and buggy is the romantic way to travel along the Costera. You can flag down an open carriage decorated with balloons late in the afternoon. They'll take you anywhere along The Strip that you'd like to go, just as they did in the mellow days gone by. The price for romance is about $12–$15 U.S. a half-hour. Fees are negotiable. Make your deal before you board.

Ferryboats operate from Caleta Beach to Roqueta Island. Some are glass bottomed, and you can arrange for an excursion to see the underwater Virgen de Guadalupe en route. Go to Caleta Beach, ask to be left off at the Pier (Embarcadero de Caleta y Caletilla), walk to the end and buy a round-trip ticket. Plain pipe-rack boats pack 'em in until 5:00 P.M. and cost about 80¢ round trip. If you want to see the Virgen and be dropped off at Roqueta, round trip costs about $1.50–$2. The trip takes about 45 minutes. The last boat comes back at 5:00 P.M.

SPORTS

Name your favorite sport and, unless it's snow skiing, you're likely to find it.

Just about every water sport under the sun is available in Acapulco. Pick out what you've always wanted to try and go to it. Waterskiing was invented here. The Acapulqueños have it down to a fine art. You can ski at your hotel or at just about any beach. Rates are approximately $20 U.S. per hour. If two people ski simultaneously, it costs the same. Jet skis can be rented for about $20 U.S. per hour at some of the Water Sports Centers on the beach. Broncos, one-person motor boats, are available on the beach, too. They cost about $12 U.S. per hour. Scuba-diving excursions can be arranged at your hotel. The best scuba schools and excursions are at Divers de Mexico (Phone 2–13–98) downtown near the Hawaiano Yacht Dock. A four-hour excursion with lessons, equipment, and snacks costs $50 U.S. per person. If you're a certified diver it's $40 U.S., less if you have your own equipment. Arnold Brothers runs three scuba excursions per day, for experts as well as beginners. Two-and-one-half-hour trips cost $45 U.S. Snorkeling trips are also available. Surfers like Revolcadero Beach, but surfing is not big here. Snorkeling is good around Roqueta Island.

Acapulco's parachute rides are world famous. Soaring over the scene for an aerial view of it all costs about $5–$7 pesos for an eight-minute ride. Boys will give you hasty instructions and help you land. You shouldn't miss this; it's one of the greatest adventures available anywhere.

Who says you can't play tennis in the tropics? Major hotels have courts that everyone can play on. Most are lit for nighttime play. They come with another luxury: ballboys, so you'll feel like a champ. Court fees range from $8 to $16 per hour during the day, a bit more at night. Ballboys get 1,000 pesos. A one-hour tennis lesson in English is about $20–$30 U.S.

Here is a brief rundown of the tennis situation:

Acapulco Plaza: 3 clay courts; Costera Miguel Aleman across from Flamboyant Shopping Center; Tel.: 4–80–50.

Acapulco Princess: 2 indoor, air-conditioned and 9 outdoor lighted courts; tel.: 4–31–00.

Club de Tenis Alfredo's: 2 outdoor lighted courts (flexi pave); Av. del Prado 29; Tel.: 4–00–04.

Club de Tennis & Golf: Across from Hotel Malibu; Avenida Costera Miguel Aleman; Tel.: 4–48–24.

Exelaris Hyatt Continental: 2 lighted indoor courts; Tel.: 4–09–09.

Exelaris Hyatt Regency: 5 outdoor lighted lay kold courts; Tel.: 4–12–25.

Pierre Marques: 5 outdoor lighted lay kold courts; Tel.: 4–20–00.

Tiffany's Racquet Club: 5 outdoor clay courts; Av. Villa Vera 120; Tel.: 4–79–49.

Villa Vera: 3 outdoor lighted clay courts; 35 Lomas del Mar; Tel.: 4–03–33.

There are two 18-hole championship golf courses at the Princess and Pierre Marques hotels. Reservations should be made two days in advance. Call: 4–31–00. Greens fees are $31 for guests; $41 for nonguests. There is also a nine-hole public golf course, "Clubs de Golf," on the north side of The Strip across from the Elcano Hotel. Greens fees are $13 U.S.

Fishing boats can be arranged at your hotel or downtown at Pesca Deportiva near the Muelle (dock) across from the Zocalo, or through travel agents. Boats that can accommodate from four to eight persons are available at about $100–$250 U.S. per day; 8–15 persons, about $350. Tel. 2–10–99. *Cost Esmeralda* is one of the best large boats. Call 4–86–71. Excursions usually leave about 7:30 A.M., and return about 2:00 P.M. The Big Ones—sailfish, marlin, tuna, or smaller snapper, mackerel, or bonito—are all prize catches.

At Divers de Mexico, you can rent chairs on a fishing boat for $50 U.S., or rent excellent boats for $200–$300 U.S. Some are air-conditioned.

Small boats for freshwater fishing can be rented at Coyuca Lagoon at Steve's Hideaway, Cadena's, or Tres Marias.

Boat Excursions. If you don't mind making like a tourist, take a cruise around the bay. You'll see the Hotel Zone and the celebrity homes from the water. A guide will point them out.

The *ACA TIKI* sails away every day at 10:30 A.M. and returns at 2:30 P.M. You board at the Colonial Restaurant dock below San Diego Fort. You stop for snorkeling at Puerto Marques beach. Cost, $31, includes buffet and open bar. Or, you can take an evening cruise from 7:30 to 10:30 P.M. Cost, $32, includes open bar, dinner, and a show. This is a local rage! Call 4–65–70 for reservations.

The *Hawaiano Yacht* cruises the Bay, too. You stop to

sun and swim. A restaurant, bar, and cafeteria are on board. There's plenty of action and live music all the way. The afternoon cruise leaves at 4:30 P.M. and returns at 7:30 P.M. There's live music, but no beach stopover. Cost: $5.50.

The nighttime cruise is pretty, too. It leaves at 10:30 P.M. and returns at 2 A.M. There is a show and lots of lively salsa music as well as a stopover at Roqueta Island for a Hawaiian show. Cost: about $6.50. For reservations call 2-07-85.

The *Fiesta* and *Bonanza* yachts also cruise. The Bonanza has three departures per day at 11:00 A.M., 4:00 P.M., and 7:30 P.M. The daytime departures have live music and stops for a half hour at La Base for swimming. There is a pool on deck. All cruises last 2½ hours and cost approximately $5.80. There is also a 7:30 departure that includes open bar, a buffet, and a show. The price is $33.50. No Sunday departures.

Both yachts depart from the dock beside the Hawaiano, three blocks from the Zocalo. Call 2-62-62 for reservations.

Bullfights. Olé! The bullfight season is December to Easter. These may not be the finest fights you can see anywhere, but they're full of color and pageantry. They take place on Sundays at 5:00 P.M. Your hotel can arrange a ticket or you can go to the Plaza de Toros ticket window or to Motel Kennedy behind Botas Moy, along The Strip. Open 10:00 A.M.–2:00 P.M. Monday–Saturday; 10:00 A.M.–3:00 P.M. Sunday. Ask for a seat in the shade (sombra). It's expensive but worth it. Barerra seats (those by the lowest railing) are top dollar. Prices range from $8 to $10. U.S. General admission is $7.50. U.S. Novice fighters perform year round. Check the schedule at your hotel and watch for signs around town. The telephone number is 5-85-40.

Acapulco
Overview

Choosing one's favorite part of Acapulco isn't easy. The fact that trend-setting homeowners' addresses are scattered all over town is telling. It just proves that all areas are pretty and popular with someone. Though the Costa Azul and Las Brisas areas certainly have the lion's share of fashionable addresses, the grand homes of many other shakers and movers can be found all over town, stretching from Caleta to the Princess.

Acapulco's history as a resort follows the coastline. The fun began over a quarter of a century ago in an area now called "Traditional" or "Old" Acapulco at the western end of the bay. Caleta and Caletilla Beach right beside it, where the sun was said to be strongest in the mornings, were *the* places to see and be seen. The longest excursion that anyone ever took was a spin around the bay or a ten-minute trip over to unspoiled Roqueta Island for more sunning and swimming; those ferry boats are still operating for all to enjoy.

In those days, hotels were built high up on the hill so that guests could have panoramic views of the bay.

Social life centered around the hotel pool, Caleta Beach, or the Yacht Club. The grandest homes were atop Avenida Lopez Mateos and the Gran Via Tropical in the area of Coyuca 22 restaurant.

Most of the hotels were small by today's standards. A 125-room establishment was considered to be enormous. These old hotels are still in fine shape and operating. They offer some of the best buys in town. Hotel Vilia, Casa Blanca, Boca Chica, and others are within a five- to ten-minute walk or drive of Caleta Beach and within a fifteen-minute drive to The Strip's Condesa or Icacos beaches, where the center of the action is today.

The Mirador Hotel high on the hill is where you can see Acapulco's famous divers perform.

This is the tranquil, time-capsule part of town. It blends into the next small section that was the second big time hub of activity. The dock where the yachts *Fiesta* and *Hawaiano* take off is nearby where Acapulco's famous Club de Ski (waterskiing) was years ago when water skiing was a major drawing card. Places where you can arrange for water skiing, scuba excursions, and wind surfing are right here.

Acapulco's downtown area is a short distance away toward the east along the bay. The bright white cathedral with blue and yellow domes presides over the main square (Zocalo). The traditional Mexcian bandstand stands in front of La Flor de Acapulco, one of the town's oldest restaurants.

Narrow streets, some of them without traffic, spring out of this hub, and the area is filled with shops, offices, and banks. This is where you'll have to come if you need to do anything important.

Woolworth's, Sanborn's, Samy's, major banks, and the Artisan's Market are all within easy strolls. You can rent a fishing boat at Pesca Deportiva. The old-time souvenir stores across the way in the arcade are fun to browse. Come in the late afternoon and you can see the boats at the dock.

Fort San Diego, built to protect the city from pirates, is up on the hill overlooking the harbor, right next to the army barracks. It has been turned into one of the best small museums in the country. Under the auspices of Mexico City's world-famous Museum of Anthropology, it displays several phases of the state's development. Exhibits are mounted in separate air-conditioned rooms of the old fort. This new addition to Acapulco's cultural life is definitely worth a visit. Hours are 10 A.M.–6 P.M. Monday–Saturday. Closed Sundays. Admission: 180 pesos, 500–1,800 pesos for special exhibits. Tel.: 3–97–30.

There is little else of interest to tourists along this stretch of the Costera. Cruise ships dock here and much of the rest of the area is for customs and commercial shipping.

Hotel Las Hamacas marked Acapulco's next stage of expansion. El Fuerte, a nightclub that has one of the best flamenco shows in town, is just next to the property.

Hornos Beach, which edges the Costera in this section just east of the downtown, is one of the prettiest beaches you can find anywhere in the world. Though all beaches in Acapulco are public, this one is considered to be a town beach that also attracts Mexican tourists. Those people know what they're doing. This beach is shaded by graceful towering palms. Thatched-roof restaurants are dotted along the edge to make spending a whole day by the sea as easy as can be. Few foreign visitors or jet setters play here because most major hotels are now up the Costera to the east.

The Costera gets more crowded as the Hotel Zone approaches to the east. The major "everyday" shopping area causes traffic congestion. The three big supermarkets—Comercial Mexicana, Super Super, and Gigante—are all in the area. The Municipal Market is a few blocks back off the highway. This area just about ends what is today considered to be "Old Acapulco," though "old" is a bit of a misnomer.

Papagayo Park, at the Costera underpass, is where the glistening string of today's major resort hotels begins. This is the western beginning—or end—of the seven-mile stretch of seaside highway called The Strip.

Just about everything one needs to make a seaside vacation perfect can be found right on The Strip between the Acapulco Paraiso and the Exelaris Hyatt Regency

Hotels. In fact, a surprising number of visitors never venture off The Strip except to go to the airport.

Almost everyone who doesn't stay out at the Princess, or the Pierre Marques, or at Las Brisas stays at a hotel on The Strip. Some feel that "if you're not on The Strip, you're not anywhere."

Right now, the most popular hotels, restaurants, discos, and shops are all packed in along this fabulous seven miles of pure pleasure that no place in the world is able to equal. This is definitely today's action center.

Beyond the Exelaris Hyatt Regency at the eastern end of The Strip, only Felipe Zamora's exotic lamp shop, a few pretty restaurants with spectacular views, the dazzling disco Fantasy, and La Vista—a shopping and entertainment complex, light up the highway that climbs to the posh Las Brisas Hotel and residential area. You'll know when you get there. The parking lot overlooking the ocean is filled with pink-and-white hotel jeeps.

From Las Brisas to Pierre Marques very little but beautiful scenery will attract your attention. The tiny bay of Puerto Marques looks like a scene from under a tropical Christmas tree.

From the bottom of the hill out to the Pierre Marques and the Princess, and farther out to the airport, the curving highway straightens out as the land becomes pancake flat.

Right now there's little to see and do here outside of the hotels, except get gas and watch equestrians. The new Lienzo Charro is a small arena where Mexican Charros (gentlemen riders) display their skills, and Mexican fiestas with folkloric dancing, cockfights, etc. take place on weekend afternoons from about 4 to 7 P.M. Price for dinner and a show is about $12 U.S. per person.

The Princess
and the East Bay

The big, bawdy, and beautiful **Princess Hotel** is the place to stay if you want to make a quick getaway. A ten-minute ride from the airport, it's the first hotel you come to after arrival.

The Princess is a self-contained resort with gorgeous grounds and gardens and wonderful walkways leading to just about everything you'd like to do on a tropical holiday. Many guests who come and stay for a week or two never leave the premises. Just about everything you dreamed of doing under the sun is right here.

The Princess and its two towers sprawl out over an expanse of flat property bordered by Revolcadero Beach right next to its smaller, quieter sister hotel, the Pierre Marques.

The Princess is for those who like 'em big and beautiful, *and* for those who don't mind being surrounded by people who wear convention badges on their bathing suits. The good news is that there's plenty of room for all—380 acres of it!

The distinctive architectural design in the shape of an Aztec pyramid has become world famous. Proportions are grander than grand. In total there are 1,032 rooms and suites, making this the biggest hotel in Acapulco. The Marquesa and the Princesa Towers flank the main pyramid-shaped building where you can look up an impressive 16-story atrium from the middle of the lobby. All tower guests check in and out in the main building.

There are two air-conditioned indoor tennis courts ($15.60 U.S. an hour for guests; $20 U.S. for others) and eight outdoor courts ($10.50 U.S. an hour for guests; $15 U.S. for others). Rates for night play are $16 U.S. an hour for guests; $20 U.S. for others. Two 18-hole golf courses are adjacent to the property. Greens fees are approximately $31 U.S. for guests, $41 U.S. for others. You should reserve two days in advance. Major credit cards are accepted.

The pool area is one of the most beautiful in the country in a nation famous for beautiful public areas and gardens. There are two salt-water and three freshwater pools; one even has underwater music. You can stand under rushing waterfalls, swim up to the bar, cross a swinging bridge and watch the ducks and flamingos prance around as you sun. The big pool with bright yellow lounges arranged side by side in neat rows is where the major outdoor sunning and socializing goes on. The smaller pool, just to the left, is quieter and sunnier in the late afternoon.

The beach is long and sprawling, so you can always find a place to make your own. The surf is rough, though, so if you want anything more than a cooling dip, head for the pool. Horseback riding along the beach is a luxury you can't indulge in at other hotels along The Strip. Out here, you can do it every day, ride as far as the eye can see, and probably not encounter anything but birds as you gallop along.

Just about any water sport you can imagine, everything from waterskiing to deep sea fishing, can be arranged at the Sports Center, though some of the excursions may begin downtown.

There are ten restaurants, including those at the Pierre Marques next door, so you have a big choice of where to dine. Le Gourmet, the top of the line, is considered to be one of Acapulco's finest dining spots, and people from all over town come here. La Hacienda, a steak house with Mexican food, is another favorite. The Amigo Bar and Restaurant features Italian specialties.

If you feel like dancing, there are a few places to try. Tiffany's is a lively disco. The Lobby Bar has live music. Cocoloco has a Mexican Show.

Shopping in the Princess couldn't be better. Cross the bridge on the right in the main building and you'll find one of the coolest and most comfortable shopping arcades in town.

You can stay in a double room in all of this spacious splendor, Modified American Plan (breakfast and dinner, mandatory in season for $170–$250 U.S. per day. The price depends on your view.) Big spenders with big families might like to rent one of the villas.

Acapulco Princess: Box 1351, Playa Revolcadero, Acapulco, Guerrero, Mexico; Tel.: 4–31–00; U.S.A. (800) 223–1818; N.Y. State (800) 442–8418, N.Y. City, 582–8100.

Note: For all hotels in this book as well as for the Princess, all rates quoted—unless otherwise stated—are for a double room, double occupancy, and are so-called European Plan, which means no meals included in the rate. All rates are of course subject to change at any time, without notice, and are specifically for The Season (December 15–April 30, 1986). Prices for the rest of the year have generally not been set yet, but can be expected to be generally 30 to 40 percent lower than the high-season rates. Unless we note otherwise, each hotel described here accepts all major credit cards.

If you tire of the Princess's crowds and noise and long for a peaceful day at the pool and a low-key lifestyle, take the five-minute shuttle bus ride over to the **Pierre Marques,** or better, stay there and use the Princess facilities. They're interchangeable.

Over here, there are only 344 rooms and villas on a flat, beautifully landscaped ocean-front property with an 18-hole golf course and attractive duplex villas.

Double room rates range from $170–$240 U.S. Modified American Plan (breakfast and dinner included). Rooms in the duplex-villa section with ocean views and patios for private sunbathing cost $200 U.S. a day. These villas are the *pièce de résistance.*

A championship golf course is just outside the door. Three freshwater pools are partially shaded by towering palms, as are five tennis courts (lighted for night play). Miles of unspoiled Revolcadero Beach are just a few steps away, too.

Pierre Marques is really a gem. This is for those who truly want to relax and get away from it all in a tranquil setting. When you're ready for crowds and action, you can dance, dine, and play at the Princess. Shuttle buses run frequently.

Pierre Marques: Box 474, Playa Revolcadero, Acapulco, Guerrero, Mexico; Tel.: 4–20–00; U.S.A. (800) 223–1818.

These two hotels have their own brands of action far away from it all. Both are resorts that are self-contained. Outside the properties, you're on your own; there is absolutely nothing to do in the immediate area.

Keep going straight from the Princess turnoff and the Scenic Highway will lead you to Las Brisas. If you go slowly you can enjoy the view of Puerto Marques, a picturesque mini-bay where Mexican tourists and locals like to play, especially on Sundays.

Keep on winding for about ten minutes and you'll reach one of the most famous and most exclusive hotels and residential areas in the world.

Las Brisas hotel is legendary. It is not only unique, but it has also been the innovator for many facilities in the hotel industry.

If you want to live in the lap of luxury and rub shoulders with big-business magnates, film stars, astronauts, and other luminaries from the world over, this is the place for you. As long as you're a guest, it's like a prestigious private club. The public is not allowed to use Las Brisas' facilities. In season, December 15 to Easter, it probably houses more celebrities than any other place in the world.   .

Las Brisas offers the very best of tropical pampering for those who are total sybarites. You won't find conventioneers or large groups here, and there are no televisions or radios to disturb your tranquility. Three hundred "casitas," all with private or shared pools and spacious terraces and all with spectacular views of the bay, are built up a hill that begins at sea level and climbs 1,200 feet.

You get around by pink-and-white staff-driven jeeps that will come up to get you and take you to reception or La Concha on the ocean. Or, you can rent your own jeep for $45 U.S. a day, including gas.

Every day is beautiful at Las Brisas. You wake to find colorful flower petals floating in your pool, and coffee and rolls waiting outside your door. In mid-afternoon, a refreshing plate of fresh fruit arrives. Every room has a fully stocked servi-bar to provide drinks at will or snacks when you get the midnight munchies.

There are two employees to every room—and for those who want to be pampered even more, there's a health spa near the reception area for men and women. Massages, facials, manicures, pedicures, a mini-gym, and an outdoor jacuzzi where you can sip fresh juices and look out over the Bay are just part of the package.

The Las Brisas sweet life couldn't be sweeter. Men never need ties or jackets. A no-tipping policy adds to the ease with which you get around.

La Concha Beach Club on the ocean is everybody's favorite lunch spot. You can swim in salt water, sunbathe or try just about any water sport, from scuba diving, waterskiing, parasailing, and snorkeling to deep-sea fishing. Tennis courts with night lights are up on the hill overlooking the ocean.

All facilities including restaurants, shops, and disco are exclusively for guests. The shops are divine.

After dark, you can dine at Bella Vista, one of the prettiest restaurants in Acapulco, overlooking the Bay.

Innovative *nouvelle cuisine* with Mexican flair is just part of the menu. After dinner, you can dance to live music at Tulipan disco. El Mexicano Restaurant, midway down the hill, overlooks the Bay and tennis courts and serves up delicious regional cuisine nightly. Don't miss Mexican Fiesta night here, Fridays at 7 P.M.

Las Brisas, a Westin hotel, both feels and looks elegant and exclusive. Double rates are $160 U.S. for rooms with shared pools; $230 U.S. for private pools. Casitas are $230 U.S. per day. Junior suites are $277 U.S. A $10 U.S. service charge is added. Rates include Continental breakfasts, fruit baskets, and membership in La Concha.

Las Brisas: Box 281, Carretera Escenica 5255, Acapulco, Guerrero, Mexico; Tel.: 4–16–50; U.S.A. (800) 228–3000.

Madeiras, Miramar, El Parador, and Los Rancheros restaurants, the La Vista Shopping complex, and Fantasy disco offer the only nearby "action" off the premises. There will soon be a French restaurant with a view as well.

FABULOUS LA VISTA

The Centro Comercial La Vista shopping complex just down the hill from Las Brisas Hotel is a world in itself.

This is the place for serious shoppers who love good things and don't mind paying for them. Out here, you can browse and buy in beautiful surroundings and in much more comfort than you could find downtown. In fact, those who are really dedicated can make a day of it, for two spectacular restaurants and one sensational discotheque as well as a deli are located near the stores.

The complex looks like a Mediterranean village with stone streets. Everything is built on the hillside, so wandering walkways give you a sense of discovery.

El Parador at La Vista has the very best view of all the nearby restaurants—and that includes Madeiras. It's at the bottom of the complex and sits out on a promontory that affords an especially spectacular view of the bay.

It is open for lunch and dinner from 12:30 P.M. to 12:30 A.M. every day, and features the famous Spanish cuisine of a chain of Mexico City restaurants, El Parador de Jose Luis. There is a special menu for "tapas" or appetizers which are particularly good. Get a table by the railing, and you'll get more than your money's worth. Prices are reasonable. Dinner for two should be around $20.

Miramar is one of the snazziest restaurants in town. Its design and proportions as well as its view of the bay are especially dramatic. It's open for dinner only from 6:30 P.M. to 12:30 A.M. (closed on Sundays). The atmosphere is more refined than most Acapulco restaurants. Though jackets and ties are never needed, you'll want to look as pretty as the place.

You should begin your evening with a drink at the bar on the upper level. It shows off the amazing architectural design at its very best. Rushing waterfalls tumble down one side of the nautilus shaped building. The elegant and romantic decor and view have already made it a popular choice for wedding receptions and parties.

The continental cuisine is prepared by European-trained chefs. Delicious chilled cream of nut soup and seabass mousseline are wonderful ways to start off a meal that can end with surprises like white chocolate mousse or chocolate covered melon balls.

The hours of 8:30–9:30 P.M. are prime time, so it's best to reserve in advance. The number is 4–78–75 or 4–78–74. Dinners run around $15–$20 U.S. per person but the setting makes it worth much more!

The soon to be opened **Miramar Deli,** just below the restaurant, will offer delicious delicacies and snacks to eat on the premises or to take out.

Shopping is sensational. Spacious, air conditioned, top-of-the-line stores are fun to browse and comfortable to shop in. Some are exclusive in Acapulco. Others have downtown branches. All offer well displayed, high quality merchandise.

Stores are generally open 10 A.M.–2 P.M. and 5–9 P.M. every day but Sunday. Marietta's, one of the best shops in town, is especially attractive out here. Beautifully carved wooden doors lead to two levels of dresses and accessories for women. Men's clothes are on the lower level. Oré, Tane and Aries, a super chic trio, share an imposing shop at the entrance. Tane features some of the most beautiful decorative silver items and jewelry in the country. Though the selection is small, it's worth a look. Aries leather goods are also famous nationwide. The clothes are original designs that can be worn anywhere in the world, but you'll pay more for them than you might in other parts of the country—and in some cases, prices exceed what you would pay at home, so shop carefully.

Gucci has a spacious store with a large selection. If you can't find what you're looking for downtown on the Costera, you might find it here. Benny's, one of the best men's shops in town, offers fine men's sportswear in attractive white tropical decor. Oceano Pacifico displays good unisex sportswear, beach towels and other beach paraphernalia in a clean modern setting. Thelma, an all time Acapulco favorite, also has a small shop that offers ready to wear as well as made-to-order fashions. Suzette is an attractive jewelry shop. Fantasy, at La Vista (see *Night Life* chapter), is one of the world's most dazzling discos. You dance with a knockout view of the Bay as a background and that's only the beginning.

There is a taxi stand at the complex, otherwise restaurant or store personnel can call one for you. Fare back to the strip is approximately 1,500 pesos.

The Strip

"The Strip" is the wide and wonderful Costera Miguel Aleman, which most people simply call "The Costera". Along this wide, crowded highway that takes the curves with the coastline all around the bay, from the end of the Scenic Highway to Caleta Beach, you can eat everything from tacos to caviar, drink everything from tequila to champagne, and buy everything from light bulbs to diamonds.

The hotels, restaurants, discos, and boutiques that line the avenue are legendary, and so are some of the people you'll see walking along.

The **Exelaris Hyatt Regency** hotel and **Plaza Icacos Mall** get things off to a rolling start just beside the Naval Base, which is easier to see from atop the hill than it is from street level.

The hotel, housing 694 rooms and suites, treats vacationers as well as businessmen with service and effi-

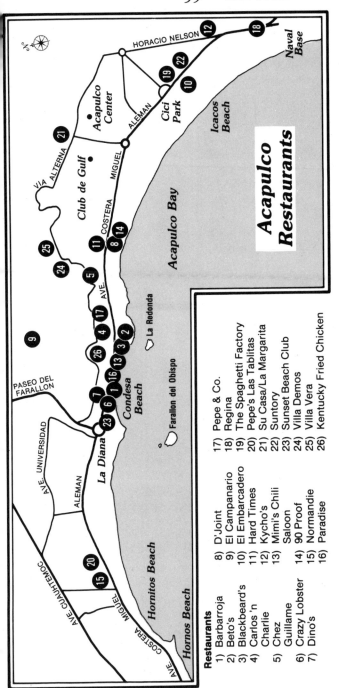

Acapulco Restaurants

Restaurants

1) Barbarroja
2) Beto's
3) Blackbeard's
4) Carlos 'n Charlie
5) Chez Guillame
6) Crazy Lobster
7) Dino's
8) D'Joint
9) El Campanario
10) El Embarcadero
11) Hard Times
12) Kycho's
13) Mimi's Chili Saloon
14) 90 Proof
15) Normandie
16) Paradise
17) Pepe & Co.
18) Regina
19) The Spaghetti Factory
20) Pepe's Las Tablitas
21) Su Casa/La Margarita
22) Suntory
23) Sunset Beach Club
24) Villa Demos
25) Villa Vera
26) Kentucky Fried Chicken

Acapulco Hotels, Shopping Malls

Points of Interest

Acapulco Hotels
1) Acapulco Paraiso Radisson
2) Acapulco Plaza
3) Calinda Quality Inn
4) Condesa Del Mar
5) Copacabana
6) Elcano
7) Exelaris Hyatt Continental
8) Exelaris Hyatt Regency
9) Malibu
10) Maralisa

11) La Palapa
12) El Presidente
13) Ritz
14) Villa Vera

Shopping Malls
15) Flamboyant
16) Galeria Plaza
17) Marbella
18) El Patio
19) Plaza Condesa
20) Plaza Icacos
21) La Vista

ciency. A shuttle bus connects it with its sister hotel, the Hyatt Continental, every half hour.

The Hyatt Regency is one of the hotels where the elite meet. Look for a group of top international bankers, doctors, lawyers, or professional men attending a meeting and you'll probably find them here. The Presidential Suite—and one of the precious elevators—was frequently commandeered by ex-President Lopez Portillo and his family, even though one less elevator made it a little harder on the guests to get up to any one of the 22 stories.

The Hyatt Regency also has some of the city's top hotel restaurants. La Cascada on the lower level is an elegant colonial-style Mexican restaurant where you'll be serenaded by trios and mariachis as you enjoy Mexican treats. It's open for dinner only, after 7:00 P.M., but it's worth waiting for. El Pescador, a seafood restaurant by the sea, is open for informal lunches and dinners. Tucked away just a few yards off the beach in a quiet corner, it's especially pretty at night.

Until the Acapulco Plaza came along, this was *the* hotel on the beach for affluent Mexicans and Americans. Almost all the rooms and suites have private terraces and a view of the bay, but since a few do not, ask your travel agent to specify "view of the ocean." It's worth paying for.

If you're startled by extra-loud noises, ask for a room on the west side of the hotel. Mexican Navy destroyers are parked next door at the Base, and the Navy seems to parade and maneuver a lot, especially on Sunday mornings when you may be trying to sleep off a super Saturday night.

If you like to stay at one of the best and be near—but not right in—the action, this is the place for you.

Rates for a double, European plan, range from $100 to $120 U.S. Rooms with a view of the ocean on the highest floors are most expensive.

Exelaris Hyatt Regency: Costera Miguel Aleman No.1, Acapulco, Guerrero, Mexico; Tel.: 4–28–88; U.S.A. (800) 228–9000.

Hotel La Palapa is a few doors down the beach. It sits off the highway in a quiet residential section, and is run by Best Western. It is the only hotel on the beach that offers *all* suites. There are 250 of them and all face the ocean. Each suite has a double bed, a single bed, and a sofa bed, a kitchenette, and a private terrace. The pool area is pretty and the beach is just a few steps away. This is a luxury hotel that Mexican families, Europeans, and Canadians on long stays like. The suites *are* suites but the rooms are minuscule. Rates are: $56 U.S. per night. A secret: The best manicures and pedicures in town are given at the Beauty Salon in the basement.

La Palapa: Fragata Yucatan 210, Acapulco, Guerrero, Mexico; Tel.: 4–53–63; in the U.S.A (800) 528–1234.

The area between the Hyatt and the Acapulco Centro de Convenciones is relatively uncongested. The new Plaza Icacos Mall has added some excitement to it. Regina's, an upscale restaurant upstairs, has an air of refinement.

By day, this area doesn't have the constant flow of sidewalk strollers that other areas have, because there are so few stores. The only interesting shops are the brand new Guess boutique and AFA, Artesanias Finas Acapulco, the crafts "supermarket" behind Baby O, a block off the Costera on the corner of Horacio Nelson and James Cook.

The only other daytime traffic is going to CiCi, the children's water-oriented amusement park, to the Secretaria de Turismo, or to Pipo's, a popular downtown seafood restaurant that opened a branch "uptown." All are within easy walking distance.

Nighttime brings an about face to this part of the Costera. This area becomes one of the liveliest, most heavily populated parts of town after dark. Baby O, the numero uno disco, Bocaccio, and Magic, three of the super eight, are all relatively close together here.

Some of the town's most popular restaurants are within walking distance as well. Embarcadero, which specializes in Polynesian food in an exotic setting, Suntory, the best Japanese restaurant in Acapulco, The Spaghetti Factory, Tipsy Bar, and Chippendale's, which offers a male strip show, are clustered nearby within an easy five-to ten-minute stroll. For those who like salsa rhythms, Nina's is just a bit farther down toward the Centro de Convenciones, whose fountains light up the night.

The Acapulco Centro de Convenciones, which everybody calls the "Centro," is amazing. It has performed its own, now-you-see it, now-you-don't magic act. A short while ago, it was a glittering entertainment complex. You got more than your money's worth from the minute you stepped off the Costera and walked in. Now, the entertainment is gone. Only a skeleton number of services are still operating, and all of those are on the lower level. The Post Office and the Telegraph Office (the telephone office is closed) are open from 9 A.M. to 3 P.M. Monday–Friday. The stores, including the Cielito Lindo boutique and Gema Pineda for leather goods, are open from 9 A.M. to 5 P.M. on weekdays. The rest of the magnificent center is used by conventioneers only.

The stretch of the Costera between the Centro de Convenciones and El Presidente Hotel is relatively quiet, too. A good portion of the highway is lined with the sprawling Centro Deportivo sports complex. To give you an idea of how big it is, this complex includes a pretty, well-groomed nine-hole golf course.

There's a geared down, tropical pace around here. Tabasco Beach, next to the Malibu Hotel and the new Fandango Beach Club are the only spots where the noise level shoots up several decibels. Almost all of the rest of the action on this stretch lies off the Costera except for Ana's, Bambu, Fiorucci, and Esteban's.

Two of Acapulco's best-kept hotel secrets are also here: the Elcano and the Malibu.

The **Elcano Hotel** is off the highway and on the beach in a beautiful seaside setting that seems far away from traffic noises and hustle bustle.

This is a bit of Old Acapulco right on the Costera. The 140 rooms are nothing to rave about, but they're clean, spacious, have cable vision and a view of the bay. The location is great. So is the seaside restaurant, which is open to all. It's a timeless oasis just a few steps up from the sand where you can linger over a peaceful lunch accompanied by the sound of the waves and undisturbed by loud music or beach vendors.

Food here has a Spanish flavor. They're famous for paella, Spanish-style onion rings—not fried, just marinated—and Spanish seafood dishes. Fried octopus is one of the mouthwatering appetizers that bring people back again and again.

This is a place where you can luxuriate over a meal as long as you like, but if you're seeking tranquility as well as more than reasonably priced delicious meals, don't come on Sundays, when Mexican families bring their children. Rooms cost about $50 per night.

Elcano: Costera Miguel Aleman, Acapulco, Guerrero, Mexico; Tel.: 4–19–50.

The **Malibu Hotel,** a few yards down the block, is a time-share hotel whose 80 rooms can be rented if owners are not using them. It's an attractive small hotel on The Strip and has only six floors of spacious octagonal rooms with balconies in two towers. Each room has cable vision. This dream of a hotel is a good place to know about. Television can be rented for a minimal amount (less than $2) per day.

Rooms cost $60 U.S. per night. There is no room service for breakfast. Breakfast and lunch are served downstairs at Tabasco Beach after 9:00 A.M. 90 Proof, a popular restaurant in the front yard, is open for informal dinners that are really good. Try the chicken or beef "fajitas."

Malibu: Costera Miguel Aleman, No. 20, Acapulco, Guerrero, Mexico; Tel.: 4–10–70.

The Tabasco Beach restaurant is pretty, and so is its tiny bar overlooking the ocean, just below D'Joint Fandango Beach Club, which is slated to be a mini Paradise Restaurant. It has a great view from two floors, live music at lunch and dinner, and an anything-can-happen ambience. A small zoo is scheduled to open soon. Tel.: 4–80–24.

The cylindrical 358–room **Calinda Quality Inn** towers over this area. This is a four-star hotel on the beach that Mexican families and big groups like. Just about everything about it is moderate—size of rooms, pretty pool, three restaurants, two bars, etc.—except for the night club. Banneret is one of the liveliest nightclubs in town. There are two big shows nightly and three dance floors to show your stuff on. Rates are about $75.

Calinda Quality Inn. Costera Miguel Aleman No. 1260, Acapulco, Guerrero, Mexico; Tel.: 4-04-10; U.S.A. (800) 228-5151.

Offices of Aeromexico and Mexicana are above VIP's Coffeeshop nearby. Fiorucci, Mando's, and a branch of Marietta's are the best boutiques around. Popular places like D'joint and Hard Times restaurant light up this part of the Costera at night. Le Dome is the only major disco here. Favorite restaurants like Chez Guillaume and Villa Demos are just up the hill off the Costera.

The **Villa Vera,** one of Acapulco's snazziest hotels, is just up the hill on Lomas del Mar, a quiet street in an exclusive residential section five minutes from the Costera. The full name is the Villa Vera Hotel and Racquet Club, and that's just what it's all about—tennis in a sleek and elegant clublike setting.

The Villa Vera began as a private home in the late 1950s. The gregarious owner then began to build suites and villas on the hillside to accommodate his guests. Later, more modest rooms for tennis players were added down below near the courts, and so the hotel began.

It was a winner from the very first moment, and launched several Acapulco "firsts." Villa Vera not only had the first swim-up bar in town but also pioneered the first rooms with private pools.

Everything about it is usually plush and easy on the eyes. So are the guests. Affluent, discriminating travelers from all over the world love this place and reserve for the next year on the day they leave.

The age range is about 25–50, and there are no children to spoil the fun or disturb the peace. You can have as much privacy or as much company as you like.

Each of the rooms or suites is different. Fifteen have private pools. Regulars sometimes reserve a specific room number when they book. All rooms are spacious, all have TV and big marble baths.

The pool and the restaurant are where to go when you want company. The pool area is one of the liveliest to be found anywhere. The friendly camaraderie makes you feel as if you're a privileged member of a private club. But think twice before you suit up. Everyone who suns, dines, or drinks around the pool seems to take special care of his or her body.

The pool and the restaurant are open to the public, but only after hotel guests and those from the sister hotel, Maralisa, have been accommodated.

The pretty restaurant has three beautiful views—the bay, the pool, and the people. It's one of the most popular and elegant places in town to linger over lunch or dinner. Lunch is big and brassy and often full of celebrities. Dinner is quiet with a cool breeze up on the hill and a view of twinkling lights around the bay. Soft piano music adds to the romance. Excellent meals are prepared by European-trained chefs. To take in the scene, get there early and eat slowly.

The most energetic aquatic event is swimming up to the bar. However, tennis here is a different matter. Serious games and tournaments take place on the pretty courts, which are three of the town's best. Tennis promotions are scheduled year round. Competitions for the Miguel Aleman Cup and the Teddy Stauffer Cups are held here annually.

It probably takes about ten minutes to walk down the hill to the Costera, but most of the guests at the Villa Vera leave the property only to shop or to go to a disco.

Rates for double rooms, European Plan, range from $92 to $52 U.S. per day in season; suites range from $187 to $202. U.S. The reason for the big spread is that all rooms are different.

Villa Vera Hotel and Racquet Club: P. O. Box 560, Lomas del Mar, 35, Acapulco, Guerrero, Mexico 39690; Tel.: 4–03–33; U.S.A. (800) 421–0767.

Anyone who wants to go the beach can comfortably do so by taking a five-minute taxi ride down to the Villa Vera's sister hotel, the **Maralisa.** This pretty hotel is a find, with plenty of unspoiled charm. It's not as glamorous as its older sister, but its location is tops (almost beside the Acapulco Plaza, just off the Costera on Avenida Enrique El Esclavo), and its small seaside restaurant is enchanting. Rooms in the main building are big but plain. Newer rooms around the two small pools look more appealing, but they are also noisier. Each of the 90 rooms has television.

For the moment, this is a four-star, not a five-star, hotel, but the location can't be beaten and the price is right: $60–$70 U.S. for a double, European Plan. Ask for a room looking south with an ocean view or west with a city view. Rooms on the east side overlook a large pool and the wall of the building next door.

Mexicans, Canadians, and Europeans are fond of this family-oriented place, which is slated to be turned into a deluxe gem. It's more than halfway there already. Maralisa guests (adults only) can use Villa Vera facilities if they can tear themselves away from the beach long enough to go up the hill. To make things even better, Maralisa is within easy walking distance from some of the major discos and restaurants.

Maralisa: Box 721, Enrique el Esclavo, Acapulco, Guerrero, Mexico; Tel.: 5–66–77; U.S.A. (800) 233–4895.

Back up on the Costera, Hotel El Presidente is across from Acapulco Joe.

The Costera's peace and quiet come to an abrupt halt at El Presidente Hotel. From El Presidente on, the action accelerates. The stretch from El Presidente to the Diana Traffic Circle just past Eve disco is strictly in overdrive. There's never a dull moment here. This strip of high-powered, nonstop action provides one of the most highly concentrated areas of pure unadulterated seaside resort fun in the world.

Acapulco's major shopping area—the place to browse, the place to buy, the place to watch passersby—as well as the merchandise—is between El Presidente and the Condesa del Mar Hotel. Some of the most popular world-famous restaurants are here, too, between the Condesa del Mar and Eve Disco.

El Presidente and Americana Condesa del Mar are the two major hotels along this strip. Coincidentally, their facilities are interchangeable. The walk between the two should take about five to eight minutes, but absolutely no one does it in that short a time. The windows, the stalls, the shopping arcades, and the other strollers are irresistible and must be viewed.

El Presidente launches the highest concentration of popular shops and malls and has one of the leading rooftop restaurants. The Condesa del Mar is at the beginning of the string of Seaside Siren restaurants that winds up at Sunset Beach Club and Eve. A few of the most popular hangouts are across the street from the Condesa.

It was only a few years ago that the Costera began at **El Presidente.** This was the most prestigious luxury hotel on The Strip. Physically, it hasn't changed much since it was the Big Star of the Costera. Proportions are still grand. The pretty medium-sized pool overlooking the beautiful stretch of beach is still where everybody congregates.

There are 422 spacious rooms and three restaurants. The clientele is a mix of Americans and Canadians, mostly groups. It's also a long-time favorite of the affluent Jewish community from Mexico City.

Rates run from $80 to $85 U.S. a day. A full American breakfast is included.

This is a great place to stay if you want to be minutes away from the action but not right *in* it.

El Presidente: Box 931, Costera Miguel Aleman, Acapulco, Guerrero, Mexico; Tel.: 4–18–00; U.S.A. (800) 228–3278.

The stores and boutiques around here on both sides of the street make shoppers salivate.

Gucci is almost across from the front entrance. Franco's, Favian, and Emil's are a few doors away.

El Presidente guests also get first crack at Acapulco Joe's gear, as they live closer to the store than anyone else does and can easily pop in to check out new merchandise arrivals every day. Ruben Torres, Stern's Jewelers, the San Francisco Silver Shop, Maraca, and Ronay Jewelers help build the crescendo to the arcades that house Sergio's, Istar, Benny's, Acapulco Pacifico, and Dancin', which are the grand and glorious finale of the area's shopping nirvana (see the shopping chapter).

Carlos 'n Charlie's, Pepe & Company, La Hacienda, and Kentucky Fried Chicken restaurants keep the action going along this little piece of the Costera far into the night (see the restaurant chapter).

On the sea side of the street, a lot of the merchandise is outdoors, displayed on the walls or on the sidewalks, and most of the buildings are condominiums.

Sanborn's, on the top of the "hill," is a reliable place where a drugstore, sundries, souvenirs, records, tapes, a bakery, and a restaurant can be found under one roof.

The action–packed **Americana Condesa del Mar Hotel,** which everyone calls the "Condesa," is close by, ending the most congested shopping area in town, and beginning the famous string of restaurants that helped build Acapulco's fame and fortune.

If you like having a lot of people around, this is the place for you. The Condesa is an establishment known for being social. There never seems to be a quiet moment in its wide, open lobby. It's difficult to figure out where the Costera ends and the hotel begins. A roof is your only clue, as there are no walls and no front door, only a front desk. Back-to-back charters and other groups seem to check in and leave around the clock. Lounges in the pool area are inches apart, but the pool is so pretty that you can almost forget that. Its very edge overlooks Condesa Beach. If everyone around the pool jumped in at once, the overflow would spill into the ocean.

Five restaurants and three bars keep you busy. Happy Hour in the Lobby Bar is one of the town's leading daily social events. When you ask a local where the "action" is (i.e., where you can find a new friend for an evening on the town), young and old alike will tell you to come here. Twofers of rum punch and ready-mixed margaritas are served in water glasses between 5:00 and 6:00 P.M., but most people don't pay much attention to the contents of the glass. The music, the meeting, and the momentum grow as the evening progresses. Even out of season the crowd at the giant bar spills out into the street. That's just about where you have to go if you want to find out what someone's name is. The only time that you can talk at tables is when the band takes a break. Rates range from $90 to $100 U.S. per night. Full American breakfast included. All rooms have a view of the ocean. Those that face south have the best views. Facilities are interchangeable with El Presidente.

This is the place to stay if you like to be right in the middle of the action. The beach is a two-minute walk away. More than a week's worth of things to do is nearby. The best boutiques and a handful of the best restaurants are within easy walking distance. You'll never have to get into a cab unless you want to go to Baby O or downtown.

Condesa del Mar: Box 933, Costera Miguel Aleman No. 1220; Acapulco, Guerrero, Mexico; Tel.: 4–26–03; U.S.A. (800) 228-3278.

The area between the Condesa del Mar and the Diana Traffic Circle is a nice mix of good shopping and sensational dining. Boutiques in the Plaza Condesa Shopping Mall across the street and the dazzling shops adjacent to it are some of the town's finest.

Acapulco's world-famous seaside restaurants are only a few stepswest of the Condesa. Beto's gets things rolling. Blackbeard's, Mimi's Chili Saloon, and Paradise keep it going, and Barbarroja, the Crazy Lobster, and

Sunset Beach Club make sure that it doesn't stop. Late-night partiers can just roll into Eve disco.

Marti, a few doors down from Eve's disco, is one of the best sporting goods stores in the country. The new Marbella Shopping Mall next door will have several fine shops, a lively beach club, and an exciting disco overlooking the ocean.

Across the street, more shops, boutiques, and stalls try to tempt passersby. Ralph Lauren, Plateria La Paloma, Zanahoria, Mando's, and Benetton are a few of the best.

The **Exelaris Hyatt Continental Hotel,** west of the circle, kicks off the last portion of The Strip with fanfare. Most facilities here are interchangeable with the sister hotel up the Costera, the Exelaris Hyatt Regency, so guests can have the best of both.

The hotel perhaps uses space more lavishly than any other hotel in Acapulco. It spreads out over what looks like two or three city blocks. The sprawling marble lobby is a wonderful place to cool off. So is the attractive air-conditioned shopping mall.

Twenty thousand square meters of lush gardens link the huge meandering pool and the beach. Ever since the days when this was a Hilton, the pool has been one of Acapulco's prettiest. "Fantasy Island," which is real, is right in the middle.

The hotel has undergone a 16-million-dollar renovation program, and it shows in the 435 rooms in twin fourteen–story towers. All of them have private balconies and a view of the ocean. Those who like to be as near to their sunning areas as possible can stay in the lanais or cabins near the pool.

La Joya is the only open-air rooftop hotel restaurant where guests can truly dance under the stars; there's nothing between you and the beautiful view of the bay. It's open in season only.

If you can't find what you want in the hotel shopping

mall, chances are good that you'll find it just across the street in Centro Comercial El Patio or Flamboyant Shopping Centers or in the Galeria Plaza Mall.

The Continental has a faithful following of American guests who used to come here when it was a Hilton. Today, Canadians, Mexicans, and a small spattering of Europeans have joined them.

Double rooms range from $85 to $100 U.S.

Exelaris Hyatt Continental: Box 214, Avenida Costera Miguel Aleman, Acapulco, Guerrero, Mexico; Tel.: 4–09–09; U.S.A. (800) 228–9000.

The Continental and the Acapulco Plaza, just a few doors away, share one of the very best locations in town. They're within easy walking distance of most of the major restaurants and discos along The Strip, and those that you can't walk to are minutes away by taxi. The area immediately outside is relatively quiet. Malls are just off the Costera, so the sidewalk there isn't congested. The only real crowding comes at night when patrons of the discos Cats, Jackie O, and Midnight need to park.

The brand-new **Acapulco Plaza** is a grand and glorious world in itself. It's the newest and largest hotel gem on the Costera, and promises to join the Hyatt Regency in becoming one of the town's very top hotels for businessmen and -women. It's a dream come true of a full-service self-contained resort right on the Costera. It has everything you want or need to make a tropical vacation perfect on the premises.

One thousand beautifully furnished rooms and suites are located in three impressive giant towers. Everything—the pools, the public areas, bars, restaurants, etc. —is on a grand scale. However, the most surprising thing about it all is that despite the proportions and the large number of people that the hotel can accommodate (almost as many as a small town) it actually manages to evoke an intimate feeling and to offer personal service.

Everyone from the elevator man to the front desk staff has a genuine friendly smile and a warm greeting. You feel as if you've made a whole new group of friends as soon as you've been here for a couple of days.

There are 508 luxury rooms in the main hotel tower and 502 suites (some have small sunken living rooms) in the Diana and Catalina Towers beside it. Rooms in the main building are $110–$125 U.S. The time-sharing suites in the Towers are $125–$140 U.S.

There are two huge pools between the towers. Both are bathed in sunshine at least part of the day. Those who want uninterrupted sun all day long can go down a few steps to the beach in a matter of seconds.

The open lobby bar and lounge, with frequent live entertainment, is only one notch down from the Condesa del Mar's in action quotient. Rooms are attractively furnished and have individual climate control, along with well-stocked service bars and television-radio sets.

Anyone who wants to get away from the children and the crowds and to relax in a quieter, adult atmosphere can pamper himself or herself at the Oasis on the mezzanine level. At this secret hideaway for sybaritic adults, you can sun, swim in two pools, have a massage or a steam bath to get last night's kinks out of your body, float around in two jacuzzis, or just have a drink and a snooze on one of the comfortable lounges.

Practically any water sport you'd like to try can be arranged at the Water Sports Center. Everything from jet skis to broncos can be rented, and parachute rides take off from morning till night. There are four tennis courts on top of the Galeria.

This is an especially great place to shop. A glittering two-story ultra-modern 50-store shopping complex called Galeria Acapulco Plaza has just opened. This is the sole location in town for some of the shops. You don't have to leave the premises to get some great bargains. Other fine boutiques line the entrance from the street, and a few more are located inside.

To make things even better, room service is the best in town. This is one of the few places where service is not only prompt, but the food is delicious. When they say that breakfast will arrive in half an hour, it does, and the eggs are warm, the coffee is hot, and the orange juice is freshly squeezed.

The hotel restaurants are all good, too. El Morro for seafood, Los Arcos for Mexican food, Maxmillian's for gourmet food. The Lobby Bar is one of the liveliest in town. Papacito's Last Call & Barbecue in the Galeria Plaza serves up some of the best margaritas in town and tasty Mexican snacks. It is plush and comfortable with live music all night, 7:00 P.M.–4:00 A.M. Other major restaurants, discos, banks, and more great shopping are just a few minutes' walk away.

In spite of the fact that this is really a small city, you'll rarely feel crowded once you've checked in. The Acapulco Plaza is truly amazing.

Acapulco Plaza: Box C-88, Costera Miguel Aleman No. 22, Acapulco, Guerrero, Mexico 39869; Tel.: 5–80–50; U.S.A. (800) HOLIDAY.

The finest art gallery in town, Galeria Rudic, is right across the street and so is Fast Jeep Rentals, in case the spirit moves you to go for a sudden spin.

Pepe's Las Tablitas, and La Fogata de Charly, two of the biggest, tastiest dining bargains in town, are a few blocks down the Costera, and so is Ron Lavender, Bachur and Associates (upstairs at Costera Miguel Aleman 155 across from the Dancing Cow), the place to go if you want to rent a villa. Call Ron Lavender, an American, at 5–71–51. Villas offer privacy, service, and tranquility. Almost all have beautiful pools and many have views of the bay. Most come with cooks and servants. If they don't, it can all be arranged. Prices vary for size and location. One to three couples can share. Three-bedroom condominiums average $225 U.S. per day.

This is also the area of the Maralisa Hotel, just off Enrique El Esclavo Street. And don't forget Normandie, *the* French restaurant of Acapulco. It's nearby, too.

The Ritz and the Acapulco Paraiso Radisson hotels have excellent locations on the western end of The Strip.

The **Ritz Hotel** caters to groups, to Mexican families, and to South Americans, Canadians, Europeans, and Americans who don't want to pay top prices to stay on the strip. The entire place has just undergone a multi-million-dollar renovation which has given it a more elegant look and feel. The 279 rooms are relatively small but all have an ocean view. The pool area is spacious and pretty and the staff is friendly. Two super seaside restaurants and Cheers, a video bar, have made it even more popular. They're doing something right. Many guests come back season after season. Average room rate is $80 U.S. per day.

Ritz: Box 259, Costera Miguel Aleman y Magallanes, Acapulco, Guererro, Mexico; Tel.: 5–75–44; U.S.A. (800) 854–3548.

The **Acapulco Paraiso Radisson Hotel,** Costera Miguel Aleman 163, was the Marriott until a year ago, has just redecorated and reopened, and promises to be a big success.

Its 442 rooms and hallways are now carpeted throughout. Bamboo furniture with modern lines is upholstered in soft pastels. Every room has a private balcony, a servi-bar, and color TV with satellite programming. It has a pretty poolside restaurant and the rooftop restaurant, La Fragata, is one of the best in town. Rates are $70–$80.

There is a sprinkle of shops around the Ritz and the Acapulco Paraiso, but none are of note. If you want to do any big-time shopping, you'll have to walk east to the Galeria Plaza or El Patio shopping plazas or take a taxi to the boutiques between the Condesa and El Presidente.

From the end of The Strip west to the downtown area there's little to see or do unless you go to Papagayo Park or to one of the supermarkets. This area is really used mostly by Mexican visitors. The beaches along here are knockouts. This is one of the few stretches where graceful palms provide shade.

Downtown and
Old Acapulco

Downtown is for those curious travelers who would like to know what makes this tropical town tick, for those who want to shop where the natives do and see how they live, and for anyone who has to go to the doctor, dentist, or see an important banker or local offical. Unless you shop at Mercado de Artesanias, rent a fishing boat or go diving, you may never see downtown at all.

The action is around the Zocalo, the main square. Narrow streets—some of them closed to traffic—and malls spring out from this hub. The sparkling white Cathedral, Nuestra Señora de la Soledad, with its bright blue and yellow domes, is one of the most photographed sights in town. The exterior is the photogenic part. There's very little of interest to visitors inside. San Diego Fort, with its beautiful museum, is a few miles east up the road.

If you want to see a bit of local hustle and bustle, walk from Sanborn's on the corner, one block away from the Zocalo, to the Mercado de Artesanias (see directions

57

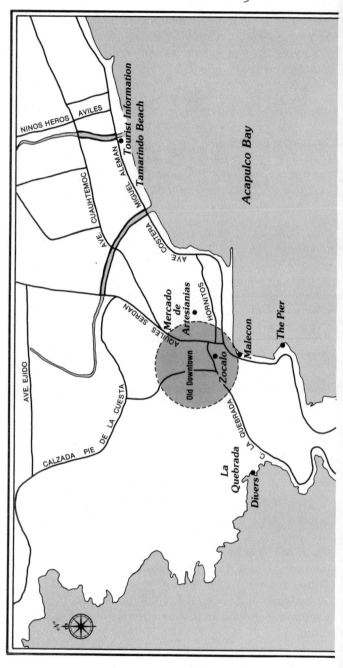

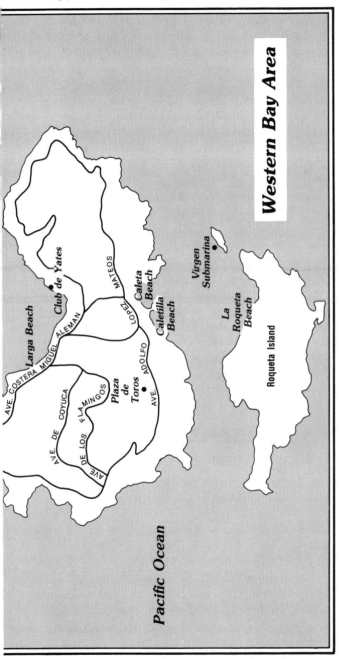

Western Bay Area

Pacific Ocean

Larga Beach
Club de Yates
AVE. COSTERA MIGUEL ALEMAN
LOPEZ MATEOS
Caleta Beach
Caletilla Beach
AVE. ADOLFO
Plaza de Toros
AVE. DE COYUCA
AVE. DE LOS FLAMINGOS
Virgen Submarina
La Roqueta Beach
Roqueta Island

in the Shopping chapter). Or eat at Pipo's famous sea-food restaurant, No. 3 Almirante Breton, or at Picalagua at No. 19 Benito Juarez.

The place to rent a fishing boat, Pesca Deportiva, is just kitty-corner from Sanborn's, beside the seaside monument commemorating the great Mexican heroes. Your chances of catching a game fish that weighs more than 100 pounds are excellent. Boats cost approximately $100–$250 U.S. per day. Most accommodate four to six people. Some can handle eight. You can see them on the other side of the monument at the dock (*muelle*, pronounced moo-ay-yeay). Tel.: 2–10–99.

The price includes tackle, bait, lines, and poles. You pay extra for beer and soft drinks, and you must bring your own lunch. A fishing license costs about $1 per person. Excursions start out around 7:30–8:30 A.M. and return between 2:00 and 3:00 P.M.

December through March is marlin season. The fact that taxidermy can be arranged makes hope spring eternal in any dedicated fisherman's heart. Reservations should be made at least one day in advance. If you come down here to make the reservation in person, you'll probably save money.

OLD ACAPULCO

Old Acapulco is where the fun began over 30 years ago. The hotels high on the hill—Casablanca, Bel Air, Vilia, etc.—were once the "in" places to stay. Today, the same places are still there, offering low-cost respite and tranquility a few miles from the action; Old Acapulco is a 12–15 minute ride (about $1.50) from The Strip.

A multi-million-dollar renovation program is currently underway to upgrade the area and restore the old tropical charm that so many visitors once enjoyed.

When this area was in its heyday, water skiing, crazy barefoot beach parties, and dancing to tropical music in the "Boom Boom Room," a thatched-roof dance hall on the sand, were the things to do. Everybody dressed like

Dorothy Lamour and lived it up around the clock, just as people are doing today a few miles up on The Strip.

Though the big spenders have moved, Old Acapulco —now called "Traditional Acapulco"—still has plenty to offer. Mostly Canadian and Mexican budget travelers are taking advantage of the low prices. $25–$40 U.S. will get you a small double room with a private bath and at best a ceiling fan. (Many rooms such as those in the Boca Chica Hotel have a view of the ocean.) Most hotels have their own small pools and pretty gardens.

Caleta and Caletilla "morning" (because that's when the sun is strongest) beaches, Acapulco's first hot spots, are just a few minutes' walk away. They are crowded with locals on weekends, but relatively peaceful the rest of the week. You can rent kayaks, paddle boats, and inner tubes, or sail away to Roqueta Island from the pier.

Ask the driver to let you off at the Embarcadero (pier) de Caleta and Caletilla. If you're driving, just follow the Costera past the Zocalo where it turns into the Gran Via Tropical, ride for about six to eight minutes until you see the Hotel de la Playa, turn right and park at the Embarcadero.

ROQUETA ISLAND

Those who want a more adventurous afternoon can take a ferry boat to Roqueta Island. A round-trip ride in a green-and-yellow ferry costs about 800 pesos at Caleta Beach. Tell the driver "Embarcadero de Caleta y Caletilla." Keep half of the tiny paper that you'll buy in a kiosk; this is your ticket back. If it's your first time, pay a bit more (about 1,500–2,000 pesos) and take the boat that detours to see the sunken statue of the Virgin of Guadalupe a few minutes away.

Roqueta has a small beach that is a great getaway during the week but crowded on weekends. The water is calm and swimming conditions are ideal. Excursion boats drop anchor here so customers can swim and snorkel.

If you're hungry, don't eat at the beach. Take the

wooden walkway to Palao Restaurant (nonslip shoes are
a must) for one of the most relaxing afternoons you
could have anywhere.

Palao Restaurant, built on the rocks overlooking
the ocean, is one of Acapulco's best-kept secrets.
Though a few excursion operators use it, it still has a
zany, primitive feeling. You get the feeling that the waiters and waitresses break into crazy songs and dances as
soon as the guests leave.

You can come for lunch, which costs about $12 U.S.
a person (boats leave from the opposite side of the pier
than those going to Roqueta Beach. Round trip costs
about $10) and stay all afternoon right through dinner.
The seafood is delicious here.

Bob around in the restaurant's delightful mini-bay
between courses, take lessons on how to blow a conch
shell from vendors who display their wares on floats, or
rent snorkel equipment and go off on your own. At night
in season there is a sassy Cuban show. Dinner, dancing,
show, and roundtrip boat ride cost about $35 per person.
Closed Mondays.

The new wooden walkway that circles Roqueta and
takes you up to its lighthouse for a spectacular view is one
of Acapulco's most sensational free pleasures. The panoramic views along the way and the thick flowers and foliage make the walk seem like a jungle adventure. Wear
comfortable shoes: Some parts are hilly.

Palao is a primitive paradise with wonderful water
views. It's also a big, welcome change from life in the fast
lane. You won't find any jet setters or big spenders here.
This is for those in the know who enjoy true informality.

The Acapulco Plaza de Toros (bull ring), is Plaza
Caletilla, just a few minutes away off the Gran Via Tropical, which is called the Costera Miguel Aleman before

you hit the Zocalo coming from The Strip. For details see the end of the General Information chapter.

If you continue on the Gran Via Tropical you'll reach the Mirador Hotel and world-famous La Quebrada, where daring divers perform several times each day. The divers played a major role in bringing international attention to Acapulco. They take death-defying leaps off a 136–foot stone cliff called La Quebrada, five times a day at 1:00, 7:15, 8:15, 9:15, and 10:30, all year long. However, the schedule sometimes changes. Have your hotel double check the hours before you go.

You can watch from a table at La Perla Nightclub at Hotel Mirador and stay on for dinner and dancing. The cover charge is 1,000 pesos per person at the bar, 1,500 at a table. Or you can go down the steps in the public area for a small admission charge, and a tip to the diver.

At night, the divers dive with torches to make the spectacle even more dramatic. But if you come during the day you can also stroll over to El Viejo Taxco shop to see the big silver selection.

For a fancier evening, you can go to see the divers and then pop over to Coyuca 22, one of Acapulco's prettiest restaurants. It's located in what was Acapulco's first grand residential section and some of Acapulco's elite still reside here. The area has a romantic sweeping view from a very different angle of the Bay.

Pie de la Cuesta
and Coyuca Lagoon

Pie de la Cuesta is the place to go after you've had enough action and want a change of pace so you can gear down to total tranquility. It's a primitive paradise—a hideaway where there is nothing to do but relax and enjoy the simple life.

It's a 15-minute drive (13 kilometers) away from The Strip. The road turns off the Costera at the new Artisans Market, winds up through Old Acapulco and around a super scenic highway that leads down to the ocean's edge. Don't stop where the boys are waving flags; go on for ½ mile and pick your place either on the ocean side or on the Coyuca Lagoon side. You can make a day of it and enjoy both.

There are no neon lights, telephones, or television to spoil your reverie.

Coyuca Lagoon could be part of Africa. It's a mirrormooth nature preserve laced with sweet-water man-rove canals and waterways. Houses are built on stilts. chool buses are dugout canoes, and bird, cricket, and rog songs fill the air.

A few waterside restaurants offer snacks and light unches and rent boats for fishing, waterskiing, or excur-ions. Conditions for waterskiing are perfect. This is the lace to try to get up on one ski if you never have before. ou can also fish for speckled trout, seabass, or catfish.

If you are making a day of it, spend it at **Tres Marias,** n out-of-the way club where you can rent a boat for kiing or excursions on the lagoon. You can ask your taxi river to come back to pick you up at an appointed hour. ound-trip fare is about $14 plus tip.

Here, far from the crowds, you can rent a boat for kiing or excursions on the for $25 an hour; Broncos two-man motorboats) cost $15 an hour. Jet skiis are also vailable.

Go with a few people if you want to get the best deal, nd get there early on Sundays to reserve a boat. You can lso arrange to do "flight sightseeing" over the lagoon n a two-man hang glider for $25 an hour.

The small restaurant overlooking the lagoon serves reat food. Go to the kitchen and order your lunch of elicious chicken or fish with a plate of quesadillas and ome mescal when you arrive. Lunch will be served at vhatever time you request. There are lounges for sun-ing and hammocks for snoozing. When you feel like salt vater, cross the street to the ocean, but beware—the vaves and undertow are rough. The sunset is unforgetta-le.

Cadena's Club Nautico, a similar club, is next door. Besides ski and excursion boats, there are facilities for ackgammon and Ping-Pong. There are also tapes and ght music here.

Those who prefer the ocean and don't mind rough vaves can cross the street to the beach. On the beach side f the road, you can lunch and spend a day on a wide tretch of beach where even the vendors and the boys vho tumble in the waves diving for pesos seem to be pure nd unspoiled. You can rent a horse and ride as far as you

can see along the beach for 3,000 pesos an hour, or lol
in a hammock with a cocoloco and listen to the waves

Sunset is the dramatic *pièce de résistance* out here. Peo
ple come from far and wide to see it. Rent a chair or ;
hammock (1,500 pesos), order a drink, and watch th
show. Some people applaud the beauty. No one wh
watches is left unmoved.

One of Acapulco's most charming small hotels is ou
here. Ukae Kim, a new suite hotel, is a little jewel. I
some rooms you have a view of the ocean from your bed
Two rooms also have Jacuzzis. Combine this with n
telephones and you have a perfect getaway for rest an
relaxation far from the maddening crowds. Nonguest
can use the Beach Club, towels, and restaurant by payin
$1.50 per person.

Casa Blanca also has overnight accommodation
with ceiling fans; they cost $15 U.S. per day with a minu
mum stay of one week.

Pie de la Cuesta isn't for everybody. It's for thos
who enjoy unspoiled natural beauty and the feel of Ol
Mexico. If you're a first timer, at least take an hour or s
off from the Costera in the late afternoon and watch th
sunset here. Go to the beach in front of one of the restau
rants; your taxi can wait. It's an experience you'll neve
forget.

Shopping

All the news about shopping in Acapulco is good. You can spend a whole day at it and still come home with enough money left for a big night on the town. Dollars go far because of favorable exchange rates, and so you can afford luxuries that you may not be able to afford at home, such as a taxi driver who will wait and carry your packages. To make things even better, glittering new shops and malls are springing up everywhere, offering high quality and a wider variety of merchandise than has ever been on the scene. Some savvy store owners have even branched into clothing for the cooler climates back home.

A good rule of thumb is: when you see something you like, buy it because no two articles made in Mexico by hand or machine are the same. Shop carefully and remember that packing in the markets guarantees that almost anything you buy will be broken. If it's big and you like it, count on carrying it home by hand. Unless you are willing to undertake a lot of complications, don't buy anything bigger than a velvet gold-trimmed mariachi hat, which will make your fellow passengers wonder about your lifestyle back home. The traditional Acapulco pirate boats and the colorful piñatas are too much for most people to deal with. In the end, they'll probably get jammed into a cardboard airline box and you might have to pay extra. Don't listen to what vendors tell you about how easy it is to check outsized items through. It's just not true.

Unless otherwise specified, store hours are from 10:00 A.M. to 1:00 or 2:00 P.M. and from 4:00 P.M. to 7:00 or 8:00 P.M. Major credit cards are accepted in most places.

MARVELOUS MARKETS

Acapulco has two great markets where handicrafts abound. Just because they're mostly open-air doesn't mean that they're cool, but once you see their staggering array of wares you'll forget about the heat. Both are a cultural experience. Bargaining is a must.

The sprawling **Mercado Municipal,** stretching over several blocks, is an Acapulco tradition. Residents depend on it for everything from fresh produce to pets. This is one of the few places in town that hasn't been altered to make it more palatable for visitors. It is a *real* Mexican market. Few tourists venture in, but doing so is worth it. You can find souvenirs, huaraches (the real ones with soles made from tires), piñatas, children's clothing, huge candles, wonderful baskets, magic potions, pets and just about anything else among the wide variety of things on display.

Christmas is especially festive. If you're lucky enough to be in Acapulco in early December, you'll get a completely different perspective on Christmas colors and decorations. And the price is more than right—many decorations are sold for pennies.

From 9:00 A.M or 10:00 A.M. to 1:00 P.M. is the best time to go. Allow at least one and a half hours for browsing. If you go by taxi, ask the driver to let you off at the flower (*flores*) section and set out from there. It's on the corner of the market at Ruiz Cortines and Hurtado de

Mendoza streets. Turn left or right from the inside end of the flower section to find souvenirs.

If you drive, come down the Costera toward Caleta, turn right when you see the sign that reads Playas S. Jeronimo, Pie de la Cuesta, Zihuatanejo, and Mercado, and keep on that road (it's narrow and congested) past bridges on the left, and then look for a parking place on the right, about a block before Ruiz Cortines. Someone, usually an old man dressed in khaki, may be there to help you park. It's okay to leave your ignition keys with him if necessary, but lock what you love in the trunk. Vendors will help you get your purchases to the car. The parking attendant should get a 600–700-peso tip when you leave. There will be a gaggle of young boys around, but this is a situation where age has rank.

El Mercado de Artesanias is easy to find. Follow the signs that read "Flea Market" or Mercado de Artesanias. It's downtown a few blocks from the Zocalo. You can walk it in a matter of minutes from Sanborn's or Woolworth's. Turn right as you leave Woolworth's and go straight until you reach the Multibanco Comermex Bank. Turn right, walk one block, turn left and walk until you see the sign for Pie de la Cuesta. Turn left until you reach Farmacia Moderna. Turn right again and you'll see the back of the market on your left.

These people don't get up early. Go after 10:00 A.M. or before 7:00 P.M. Don't overlook the open stores and stalls on the other side of the street. They look funky, but you can find some treasures and see some local color. Stores are rustic, not ultramodern, but this is the place to come for props if you ever have to whip up a costume on short notice. Hats, raffia purses, and baskets sell for less than on the Strip.

If you go by taxi, start at the opposite end where the pottery (*barro*) section is and work your way back.

This market, with its gay yellow awnings, is the Cadillac of Acapulco's open markets. It's geared for tourists, but still retains some Mexican flavor. If you look carefully you can find some pretty things among the puppets, serapes, onyx backgammon boards (which break if they're tapped), bars and blocks of Sirena, the famous Acapulco coconut soap (*jabon de coco*), and the rest of the souvenirs. Spirited bargaining is in order here, especially if you buy more than one item in a stall. Begin by offering half of what the vendor is asking.

You can watch people drawing and painting pottery. If you have a few days, you can order a plate, vase, or lamp base to match your décor. Chances are that you won't be able to put water in the vase because the plaster is too porous, but you can be sure that it will look great.

For those who don't like going downtown, there's an "uptown" handicrafts market called **Noa Noa,** on the Costera at the turn-off for the Municipal Market at Calle Hurtado de Mendoza. It's a clean, mini-version of the downtown market, with the same array of serapes, embroidered dresses and other typical souvenirs that appeal to all tastes, displayed in 150 stalls. You won't see the profusion of pottery, or anybody painting here, though. For that you have to take the trip downtown.

Artesanias Finas de Acapulco, one block off the Costera behind Baby O disco at the corner of Horacio Nelson and James Cook, is a handicrafts supermarket featuring things from throughout Mexico. They have more handicrafts than you ever dreamed existed— 13,000 square feet of them. Prices are fair, and what is lacking in quality is there in quantity. This is a good and practical place to buy and one of the only places where you can buy souvenirs with major credit cards. Hours are 9:00 A.M. to 7:30 P.M, Monday-Friday and 9:00 A.M. to 2:00 P.M. on Saturdays. Unlike most other places, they're also serious about packing and arranging for shipping.

For the moment, there is only one good folk-art store. It is above the silver shop in Las Brisas.

THE MAGNIFICENT NEW MALLS

The glittering new shopping malls almost outdazzle the discos. They make buying and browsing cooler, more comfortable, and more convenient than ever before and bring many major shops just a few steps away from your front door.

Modern new stores featuring sportswear, swim suits, accessories, decorative items, and jewelry shops add more sparkle to an already sparkling scene.

You'll find the several new malls almost evenly spaced throughout town. Many include branches of stores that were once found only on the Costera.

Some are not fully open at this writing, and a few more are under construction. But so far, the news is nothing but good. The new malls have brought higher quality goods and higher styles suitable for wear any place in the world to Acapulco.

Here they are from east to west:

La Vista is the posh shopping mall for residents of the Las Brisas section and hotel. It looks like a pretty, well-groomed Mediterranean town built on a hillside overlooking the Bay.

Attractive **Plaza Icacos** is at the bottom of the hill next to the Navy Base. **Lorea,** a lovely shop featuring furniture and unusual decorative items, and **Mando's** are already operating, along with **Holanda** for ice cream and Regina Restaurant upstairs.

Plaza Condesa, across from the Condesa del Mar Hotel, is built on a hill on three levels. It also has several restaurants, including Aldo's, an Italian restaurant, and Trapiche, a sassy snack bar. The Flying Indians of Papantla perform in the afternoons. Tickets cost about $5. **Los Sotelos** is a good silver shop.

Just below Plaza Condesa in glittering two-story locations are **Jag's, Goldie,** and **Oceano Pacifico** for sports and resort wear, **Pasarela** for evening clothes, and **DuDu** for silver and decorative items.

Marbella Mall, at the Diana Traffic Circle, promises to have another fine collection of stores very soon.

Marti, nearby, is the place to find everything under the sun that has to do with sports, from earplugs to speedboats.

The **Galeria Acapulco Plaza** is already off and running with a head start that makes it a sure winner. A few stores here, such as **Diva** and **Banana Republic,** and **Ferrini** for resort wear and **Pineda de Taxco** for silver jewelry are among the shops that can't be found anywhere else in town.

Acapulco Joe, Guess, Express, and others with branches around town are here, too.

Older malls are still going full speed ahead. Stores in the **Flamboyant** across from the Acapulco Plaza and the **El Patio** shopping center across from the Hyatt Continental offer fine selections. In general, El Patio stores are more traditional. The same pretty eyelet dresses that no one ever tires of are still here, along with more contemporary clothing for men and women at places like **Thelma's** and **Marietta's. Samatha Just, Mar y Mar,** and others in Flamboyant have trendier fashions.

Though most hotels have a collection of boutiques tucked away somewhere, the collection at the Princess outdoes them all. There are about 25 attractive stores with first-class merchandise ranging from jewelry to art. It's worth a trip out there just to shop and get a good glimpse of the hotel as well. Taxis from the Hyatt Continental to the Princess cost about 4,000 pesos one way. This is the only mall that is air-conditioned throughout. It is an indoor, uncrowded, shoppers' delight.

Familiar names that offer well-selected sportswear are there, along with Acapulco Joe, Emi Fors, Ronay, Bulgary (no relation to the renowned Italian firm) for jewelry, and Loala and Pupu for silver and decorative items.

Marietta's and the Inter-Art Gallery are the two big stars. Inter-Art is the local representative for Sergio Bustamante, the world-renowned Mexican artist who is famous for whimsical papier máché animals in gay colors and for beautifully mysterious sculptures as well. The collection here is big and good. Large animals sell for $500–$800 U.S. Smaller pieces go for from $50 to $500 U.S. Dependable shipping can be easily arranged.

Marietta's store is spacious and stocked with lots of great models for all ages, styles that can be worn back home. Cotton jumpsuits and sundresses, evening wear, summer street wear, and accessories—even wool shawls for those who are not thinking tropics—are here in profusion. They also have things for men as well. This is one of the best selections in town.

SPORTSWEAR

Attractive men's and women's resort wear is another shopping mainstay. The selection here is about as wide as you could find anywhere in the world—and the prices are better, too. It comes in all sizes, colors, models, and prices. Most is made of lightweight cotton or T-shirt material. If anyone ever managed to count it all, the quantity for women would far surpass what there is for men. You can find just about anything to wear on and off a beach, or have it made.

Anyone who says it's too hot to go downtown and have something made to order should think twice. It wasn't too hot for Henry and Nancy Kissinger, for the Baron and Baroness di Portanova, for Margaux Hemingway, Lauren Bacall, Mia Farrow, and a long line of other international celebrities.

Somehow, they've all managed to make their way to **Samy's,** a modest little hole-in-the-wall at No. 7 Calle Hidalgo, and to make their way back again and again. Just face the Cathedral, turn left at Banobras Bank, walk for two blocks and you'll find it on the left, about three doors from the corner. Samy is one of the last of a very few who still make things to measure and charge reasonable prices. A chat with him alone makes the trip worth it. He has a philosophy about everything and loves telling you about it.

Samy's marketing idea is to vary his merchandise according to who's in town. He gathers his very best things, long skirts and dresses, caftans, and elegant clothes for the November-through-Holy-Week season when homeowners, jet setters, and big spenders are in town.

After Semana Santa, he changes to merchandise that has more appeal to Mexican tourists. During summer months he features clothes for even hotter weather. Men as well as women have to keep cool, says Samy, who also makes tailor-made shirts and pants.

This wily transplanted Spaniard, who can melt your heart with smoky-voiced enthusiasm, says that he keeps on working and keeps his prices low because he loves his business. He creates a few of his own models, sprinkles in some Mexican designs, copies simple patterns, and makes things to order if your size isn't there. He'll even outfit you for a costume party if you like. Samy's mens' shirts and pants and ladies' blouses, skirts, caftans, and wearable handicrafts can be seen at leading resorts all over the world. These aren't things for the young crowd. They're perfect for over 30 trendsetters. All of these celebrities are right on target. Samy has some of the best values in town. When you see the place you may not believe all of this, but it's true. This is strictly cash and carry. The store is open from 9:00 A.M. to 1:00 P.M., and from 4:00 P.M. to 8:00 P.M. in season. It closes one hour earlier in summer. Dress prices range from $25 to $80. By popular demand, Samy may open a branch "uptown" at 21A Rocasola, just behind Pizza Hut. Call 2–16–18 to find out if it's operating.

Besides a few other souvenir stores (it's fun to browse the old-fashioned ones on the Costera at the far end of the block past the Zocalo), Woolworth's, Sanborn's, the Artisans market, and an odd shoe store, this is just about the only shopping to be done downtown.

The greatest concentration of medium-priced resort-wear stores lies on the North Side of the Costera from the Condesa del Mar to the Holiday Inn Hotel, where it's shady in the afternoons. Don't just browse the street front, go all the way back in the arcades to see great boutiques like Esteban's and Istar, or Oceano Pacifico in the Arcades under Carlos 'n Charlie's and Pepe & Co.

Acapulco Joe, opposite the Presidente on the Costera, is King of them all. Trendy, young, unisex action wear—T-shirts, pants, jackets, shirts, and jogging outfits —is stacked on high-tech shelves and moves faster than greased lightning. "Aca Joe" doesn't have to set up an export operation, nor does he have to worry about national distribution. The clientele is doing it for him. In season you'll frequently find lines waiting to get in, and even longer lines waiting at the cashier's desk. There is a branch at the Princess and at Galeria Plaza. Prices are much lower than they are back home.

Get accustomed to it. Just about any of the less expensive things you buy, and some of the expensive ones, too, will say Acapulco in a way that can't be removed. Mexicans seem to have gone logo crazy. A small ACA with or without wings is Acapulco Joe's. OP stands for Oceano Pacifico, AP stands for Acapulco Pacifico, and Ruben Torres stands for Ruben Torres. Torres is mostly for women. The others are unisex. They're all hot boutiques that offer good value. **Acapulco Pacifico** is on the Costera under Pepe & Co. **Oceano Pacifico** is downstairs on the beach side under Torres Gemelas. **Ruben Torres** is next to Acapulco Joe's. His sportswear made of T-shirt fabric that comes in delicious ice-cream colors, and those at Mar y Mar in the Flamboyant Shopping Center, and the Galeria Acapulco Plaza, are the best available. C-83 (look for the "airplane hangar" across the street just beyond El Presidente) has a good collection, too. A handful of new boutiques—Anna's, Favian, and Maraca, all on the Costera, Express, Fiorucci, and Guess—are also good.

SERIOUS CLOTHES

There are several stores that offer top-quality resort wear at higher prices.

The **Pitti Palace** in the Acapulco Plaza and in the Princess are a pair of sassy beauties. Together they offer some of the best styles and workmanship in town. They both cater to an affluent style-conscious crowd of all ages, and specialize mostly in women's clothes and accessories, for day and evening.

Esteban's on the Costera just past the Elcano Hotel is one of the most fashionable boutiques in town. He sells quality sportswear for men and women, bathing suits, dresses, belts, and accessories. High fashion leather outfits and silk and linen ensembles as well as opulent evening dresses have become a specialty. Prices are high

—anywhere from $200 to $1,000 U.S. and up—but they're still at least 40 percent less than they would be back home.

Istar, at the end of the arcade, under Carlos n' Charlie's, offers attractive high-fashion designs with European flair for men and women. You can have items made to order in no time. In general, the styles are a bit avant garde. The quality of the fabric is lighter and the workmanship is a notch down from Esteban's. But so are the prices, and they're more than worth it. Sergio, one of the best designers in Acapulco, is the man behind the scene.

Pasarela, in both the Galeria Plaza and Condesa Plaza, has top-of-the-line hand-beaded dresses and knockout evening clothes plus a dazzling array of accessories. Dress prices range from $200 to $900.

Marietta's, up a few stairs on the left in El Patio Shopping Center, out at the Princess, at La Vista, La Torre Acapulco, and the Galeria Plaza, is where many resident Acapulco women have their party and disco dresses made. Prices may seem high ($70–$90 U.S. for a cotton dress), but trendsetters swear by her. If you know how hard it is to find attractive, well-made cotton clothes in the U.S., you'll think they're a bargain. Designs range from conservative to avant garde. **Oré** in La Vista also has quality clothes and accessories.

LEATHER GOODS

In general, Mexican leather goods leave a bit to be desired. The price is right, the leather is good, but the workmanship and fittings are generally not up to snuff. That doesn't mean that you shouldn't buy leather. It's at least 40 to 50 percent less expensive than it is back home, and with patience you can find something that *is* up to snuff. If you need a good leather handbag for work, this is the place to buy. If you want a fine leather evening bag, wait till you get home.

Gucci, in El Patio Shopping Center, on the Costera

across from El Presidente, and at La Vista, is a good place to begin. The merchandise is Mexican made from Italian designs. Prices are high by Mexican standards, but not by ours. A hard-to-detect copy of a man's tasseled loafer is $60 U.S. Some of the ladies' handbags are good, too. They cost from $40 U.S. to $100 U.S..

Aries, in Las Brisas Hotel, has nice suitcases, briefcases, and handbags that are good buys. This quality store is headquartered in Mexico City. In general, workmanship is good. Purses are in the $40 U.S.–$100 U.S. range.

ART GALLERIES

Surprisingly, Acapulco has two fine art galleries: **Galeria Rudic** across from the Hyatt Continental and **Galeria Victor** nearby in El Patio shopping center. Rudic carries an outstanding collection of contemporary Mexican painters and sculptors, including Armando Amaya, Leonardo Nierman, Norma Goldberg, Trinidad Osorio, and Maria Elena Delgado. It also carries works by Diego Rivera, Jose Clemente Orozco, and David Alfaro Siqueiros. The gallery is open from 10:00 A.M. to 2:00 P.M. and from 5:00 P.M. to 8:00 P.M. on weekdays and from 10:00 A.M. to 2:00 P.M. on Saturdays. Galeria Victor, one of the world's most beautiful galleries, displays the work of Victor Salmones, a super-talented local sculptor and designer whose work has attracted worldwide attention. Hours are 9:30 A.M.–1:00 P.M. and 4:00 P.M.–8:00 P.M. every day except Sunday. **Pal Kepenyes,** a fine sculptor whose work has considerable style, exhibits in his home overlooking the Bay. He also makes exquisite jewelry. Call for a viewing appointment, 4–37–38. The house is at the beginning of Guitarron, No. 140. **Inter-Galerias,** across from Eve Disco, has a beautiful display of Sergio Bustamante's whimsical metal, wood, and *papier-mâché* sculptures. The nearby **El Dorado Gallery** carries outstanding works by one of his former employees, Mario Gonzalez.

There is another good art gallery beside Esteban's boutique.

SILVER

The State of Guerrero, particularly Taxco, which can be a day trip from Acapulco, has been one of the world's leading silver capitals for centuries, and still holds its rank today. The work of talented Mexican silversmiths is internationally famous. Look for names like Antonio Pineda and the Castillo brothers on the pieces, and you'll know that the silver is sterling, the design is good, and the craftsmanship is excellent. Disregard what street vendors sell unless you make a very close inspection for the official 9.25 sterling stamp. Much of what they sell is only silver-colored.

However, if the real thing doesn't fit into your budget, don't disregard silver plate. Mexican silver plate is particularly good. Most has at least four or more coats (*baños*) of silver. You can ask how many when you buy.

Acapulco's silver shops are not as plentiful as one might expect. Some jewelry shops, such as Emi Fors, carry attractive silver and silver-plated tableware. Three leading shops are dedicated to the shining metal, and they're spread from one end of Acapulco to the other. If you visit them all, you'll see the whole town.

El Viejo Taxco in Old Acapulco, up near the Mirador and the divers, is housed, along with some less-interesting boutiques, in a pretty, air-conditioned colonial-style building.

The collection is more extensive than anywhere else. Bracelets, rings, necklaces, key rings, and table items are here in air-conditioned profusion. Surprisingly, there is very little silver flatware here or anywhere. The sterling is guaranteed, but designs of everything across the board are definitely old style, the traditional models that veteran travelers to Mexico have been buying for years. The traditional round silver-bead necklaces, both uniform and graduated, are especially pretty and have a classic flair. If you buy several items you can ask for a discount.

Pineda de Taxco, in the Galeria Acapulco Plaza, is one of the most exciting silver shops in the country. It looks just like a silver shop should. Everything shines and sparkles. Bracelets, necklaces, earrings, and other things here come in a variety of prices that depend on the weight of the piece. These designs are more contemporary and innovative, though many popular old styles are mixed in. Ask for a discount, which will save you the tax if you buy several items. Pineda is open from 9:00 A.M. to 10:00 P.M., Mondays through Saturdays.

Pupu, in the Acapulco Princess Hotel shopping center, has some of the very best pieces designed by Los Castillo and other famous silversmiths. Designs are beautiful and whimsical. A pitcher may have a bird inlaid with copper, brass, and lapis lazuli on the handle. A bowl may be bordered by polished obsidian frogs, etc. Enamel work by Manuel Pineda, who decorated the doors of the new Basilica of Guadalupe in Mexico City, are here, too. Each piece is a unique work of art. Prices for small things begin at $35 U.S.–$60 U.S. and go up to $500 U.S. or more for larger ones.

Tane in La Vista and the Acapulco Plaza Gallery is tops. It's a wonderful place to buy exquisite gifts and decorative items that will bring a lifetime of pleasure.

Boutique Laola, in the Princess Hotel, offers attractive silver items as well.

JEWELRY

Emi Fors is a reputable shop with a lot of Acapulco tradition behind it. Mrs. Fors is an attractive Texan who has resided in Acapulco for some years. Her merchandise reflects the finest American and European tastes. Employees speak English and make selecting from small pieces to big ticket items easy. Silver and gold are guaranteed. Some of the pieces are Mrs. Fors' exclusive designs, which combine gold with precious and semi-precious stones. There's something beautiful for everyone here—and at a fair price. Shops are located at the entrance of the Acapulco Plaza and in the Hyatt Continental and Calinda Quality Inn hotels. The stores are open from 10:00 A.M. to 7:00 P.M. every day.

Other good jewelry shops, such as Hans Stern, Ronay, and Trevi, line the Costera.

ALL UNDER ONE ROOF

Sanborn's, the "everything store," is a reputable pharmacy-souvenir shop-restaurant-bakery chain that Americans either residing in or visiting Mexico have relied on for years. They carry everything from tapes, records, and sunglasses to beachwear, medicines, cosmetics, and appliances. Their line of cosmetics is just about the best around. They also have a selection of ·maps and English-language paperbacks. You can even buy postcards and stamps here. There are two branches open seven days a week, from 8 A.M. till 10 P.M. One is beside the Fiesta Americana/Condesa del Mar and the other is on the main corner of the Costera and Calle Escudero downtown. Their restaurants have the best milkshakes in town.

Woolworth's. Surprise! A big location downtown just beyond Sanborn's is just like home. It's a good place for cosmetics, sundries, and Christmas stocking gifts. Most things are Mexican made, but if you forgot anything and can't find it here, chances are you won't find it at all. Even the restaurant is U.S. style—good, quick, and inexpensive. It's open everyday from 9:30 A.M. to 8:00 P.M.

Super Super. The Super Super *is* super. It's a combination of a sprawling liquor store, produce market, deli, and department store, on the Costera, north side, across from Hornos Beach. It carries everything from shampoo to prickly pears, sunglasses, and beach towels to souvenirs, as well as just about anything else you're looking for, including the English newspapers. Their selection of Mexican wines and liquors is very good. This is a fine place to check prices on local wines and liquors. The snack bar outside serves fried chicken and hamburgers to eat there or to take out. Super Super is open from 8 A.M. to 10 P.M. daily, including Sundays. It is on the Costera, just past Papagayo Park, across from Hornos Beach at the corner of J.R. Cabrillo Street.

Gigante, nearby, is another mega "everything" store which seems to place a bit less emphasis on food and more on the kinds of things that are necessary around the house. Brands are good. Some items can't be found anywhere else in town.

Restaurants

In Acapulco, food and fun are served up on the same plate with a lot of wit and élan. The informality is deceiving, though; the menus and the shenanigans are planned with a precision and expertise that would attract the admiration of any restaurateur in the world who wants to show a profit at the end of the year.

A restaurant in Acapulco isn't only a place to eat, it's a place to laugh, a place to enjoy a beautiful view, a place to romance, and sometimes a place to drink and dance between courses. They're also places where you can get your money's worth for a meal. In general, prices are moderate, even in gourmet restaurants, especially if you stay away from imported delicacies, wines and liquors. Dinner for two in a gourmet restaurant such as Le Gourmet in the Princess or Coyuca 22 may range from $40 to $50 U.S. per person. At Madeiras, the price range is $15–$20 U.S. A big lunch or dinner for two at the seaside places or the popular hangouts averages $15–$25 U.S. At Pepe's Las Tablitas or at Los Rancheros, your bill might be under $12 U.S. for two. Most places accept major credit cards. In the end, when everything is added up, they probably deliver better value than most of the finest restaurants you can find anywhere in the world.

Even in the fussiest, most precious ones the indomitable Acapulco wit sometimes breaks through. In most of them, however, it's right out there on the table along with the food.

There is a staggering variety of dining spots to choose from, everything from informal seaside restaurants where you don't need to wear shoes to formal gourmet spots where you'll want to be dressed up. You can find just about any kind of cuisine you crave: German, Chinese, Japanese, and good old American (however, Acapulco is not the best place for the most delicate French cuisine). To make things even better, chances are that your meal will be served in a beautiful setting. Most restaurant food, except for hotels, comes out of minuscule, primitive kitchens where local chefs perform wondrous culinary miracles in cramped quarters.

Ingredients and produce are fresh daily. Most dishes are simple. When you choose a restaurant you are really choosing ambiance. Most places stick to a few versions of fish, lobster, or meat. Little of the Pacific lobster, shrimp, and snapper is caught near Acapulco; but most of it comes from the surrounding areas.

Remember, Acapulco is a place that has been catering to tourists for a long time, and Acapulqueños have their own proven formula for what makes for successful dining in this tropical port. Pranks and jokes are all part of the service, which is generally good. Often, service skills are passed down from father to son, and many of the restaurants are owned by ex-waiters and managers.

This very special kind of service might not pass muster in European or American resorts, because it is permissive, flip, and funny, and allows the waiter's personality to become an integral part of your dining experience. In fact, your waiter may play as important a role as your food in providing you with an enjoyable dining experience.

Acapulco restaurants have one other feature that makes them especially endearing: they never rush you and they won't close until the last diner leaves.

Seeing a restaurant at prime time turns a meal into

a cultural experience. People-watching in Acapulco is some of the best in the world, so even if you have to snack in order to wait until later, schedule your meals when the local scene is in full swing. If you want to eat in the better restaurants, make reservations early (one or two days in advance), especially in peak season (December–March). Don't overlook hotel restaurants, especially in season, when places tend to get crowded. They're among the few places that are air-conditioned.

Breakfast is light and whenever you want it. You might as well eat it in your hotel. Lunch, the main meal of the day, begins between 2:00 and 4:00 P.M. (though most places open at noon), and can last until 6:00–7:00 P.M. if you let it. Cocktails are usually from 7:00 to 9:00 P.M. Dinner begins at 9:00 P.M. or later. Even Mexican babies dine on this schedule.

THE FOOD

Though jokesters may have given you the impression that all dishes are filled with palate-shattering chiles, the cognoscenti of Mexican cuisine will tell you that the opposite is true. Yes, many hot-food lovers flock to Mexico specifically to enjoy the amazing variety of chiles (*habanera* is the hottest) that are yet another culinary experience. But there are endless numbers of intricate dishes to be enjoyed by those with tamer taste buds.

Seafood is an Acapulco specialty. Many restaurants have their own fishing fleets to make sure that food will be fresh every day, and no matter where you eat you'll discover that it is.

Ceviche heads the list. It's slightly warm raw fish marinated in lime juice. This is one of the least expensive seaside dishes you can get. A glass of it is often served as an appetizer. A bowl can be a meal.

Perhaps the most familiar of all Mexican food is the tortilla, a flat, round, pancake-shaped bread. They're made from cornmeal (*maiz*) or wheat (*harina*) and come in a variety of colors ranging from light beige to blue.

Most of the Acapulco varieties are the slightly heavier corn ones. Rolled with meat or chicken or cheese and baked, the tortilla becomes an enchilada. Fried to hard-crisp and broken up into pieces, it becomes a tostada. They're delicious when served with dips like guacamole or red sauce. Filled with meat, chicken, cheese, or vegetables, they become tacos. *Taquerias,* taco shops, are popular Acapulco institutions. You may pop in for a snack or make a whole meal of them. Whatever you do, the price will be right. However, unless you're outdoors, the place will probably be slightly smoky and smell of cooking oil. This doesn't seem to bother Mexicans. It only whets their appetites for a delicacy that they love.

Guacamole. If you haven't tried it in Mexico you've never tried it. This dip is ambrosia. It's made of fresh mashed avocadoes, green tomatoes, jalapeño chiles, and scallions, and served with tostadas.

Huachinango, red snapper, is delicious. If you order it you'll probably get a big one that may be the only meal you need all day. Grilled snapper is mouthwatering. Most places have garnishes that make it look like a dish from *Gourmet* magazine.

Camarones, shrimp, are big and succulent, too. They're usually prepared grilled, or in *mojo de ajo* (garlic sauce).

Langosta, lobster, is the stringier Pacific type. There's little meat in the legs and tail fins, but what there is in the claws and the tail makes up for it. Served with drawn butter and lots of lemon, it's out of this world. But, like most things that fall into that category, it's expensive.

Huachinango is really the best bargain of the three.

THE BIG SEVEN

Le Gourmet at the Princess Hotel is a class place that a lot of people make a fuss over. Some say it has the finest food in town. Others disagree, because some nights it's great and some nights it isn't. If you're willing to take a high-priced gamble on a fine meal in a plush and comfortable air-conditioned restaurant, this is your place.

It has the patina of big spenders. The setting is formal, though décor is minimal. Seats are big and soft. Service is elegant and the menu offers a wide choice of Continental and French dishes. No rock music or crowded tables interrupt the soothing deep-blue décor and the genteel atmosphere. The clientele is a United Nations of people who like to eat well. A fat-cat atmosphere prevails.

This is for the older crowd who likes to dress for fancy dinners. Le Gourmet is open every night from 7 P.M. to midnight. Follow the signs once you enter the hotel. It's upstairs on the left in the back of the main building. The reservations number is 4–31–00. Be ready to spend $35–$45 U.S. per person or more.

Madeiras is the Baby O of the restaurant scene. Everybody wants to go, but not everybody can get in. The spectacular view isn't the only reason. High on the hill overlooking the bay on the Scenic Highway (Carretera Escenica) between Las Brisas and the Exelaris Hyatt Regency, it is not only pretty on the outside but on the inside as well.

Its view and furnishings are a cut above most others. So are its prices and modus operandi, but once inside you get more than what you pay for. Definitely catering to the affluent Las Brisas crowd, the place has a decorated *Town & Country* look. So do the clientele, mostly attractive, well-dressed Americans and Europeans. This place is more formal than most other Acapulco non-hotel restaurants. You wouldn't want to come to a place that is so pretty without looking as nice as it does.

Top tables are on the lower level, but even the big spenders who reside in Acapulco claim that they don't get a chance at these tables most of the time. They're relegated to the mysterious Mexican pecking order that most restaurants in Acapulco seem to have: You have to be a known—and liked—client, a friend of the owners, or a celebrity to get a chance at the very best seats.

However, tables on the upper dining level aren't to be sneezed at. The ones around the railing are crème de la crème. The right-hand far corner (as you face the bay) is the zenith of tropical romance. You're a few feet away from the crowd but a bit hidden, and you get a delightful breeze that may not enter the main open-air dining room, which can get hot in season.

The attention to details and food presentation is extraordinary. Table settings are more than tasteful. Madeiras is associated with Los Castillo, the world-famous Taxco silversmiths; the sugar bowls and creamers, as well as some of the table settings, are their design. You can see a display of their work and buy some in the gift shop near the entrance, but the old adage applies here: The best is always expensive.

The small basket of tiny croissants that arrives at your table just after you're seated leads the way for the good things to come. These details, along with delicious food and gracious service, are what attract their discriminating clientele.

Dinners are *prix fixe*. Seatings are at 7:30 and 10:30 P.M.—and don't count on being let in if you arrive more than a half hour late.

Salads, soups, entrees, and desserts are all beautifully presented. Most items on the menu are Continental cuisine, but there are Mexican specialties like *crepas de huitlacoche* (corn-fungus crepes), which are out of this world. Dinner for two, with a Mexican wine, costs $30–$35 U.S.

Everything about Madeiras is great, once you're inside, but getting inside isn't easy. Money doesn't grease the portals if you haven't bothered to reserve. Everyone involved in the reservations process seems to be snooty. In season, reservations should be made a week or more in advance; during the rest of the year four days will do it. They have a way of mixing up names or losing them. The parking attendant even asks if you have a reservation before he'll park your car. There's no good time to get through on the phone. You just have to keep trying or leave it to your hotel. During Christmas and Easter weeks, either call from home before you come or reserve a week or two in advance.

As with Baby O, the only thing that you have to decide is whether or not it's worth the time and trouble to fight your way in.

The reservation numbers are 4–43–78 or 4–69–21. Good luck!

Miramar in La Vista shopping complex is grand scale elegance with the same view as Madeiras. You feel as if you're entering an opulent private home. The cozy bar is a knockout. Begin there, not only for a drink, but also for a view of the bay and the restaurant. Then descend the gentle steps to the spacious main dining room. This may be the most comfortable restaurant in town. Tables are far apart and there's plenty of floor space to spare so you'll never have to listen to the conversation at the next table.

Chilled nut soup, seabass mousseline, red snapper amandine, and delicious desserts such as white chocolate mousse are popular menu items. Dinner for two costs about $16–$20 U.S. with domestic wine. Miramar is open 6:30 P.M.–12:30 A.M. daily. Closed Sundays off season. For reservations telephone: 4–78–74/75.

Maxmilian's, in the Acapulco Plaza, is the best of both worlds. It not only offers fine food in a formal setting, but it's one of the few air-conditioned places in town that has a view of the ocean. It's the only fine restaurant that's almost *in* the water.

The dining room is decorated in soothing shades of soft blue. Romantic tables for two line the big glass picture windows. The décor is plush, sleek, and modern without anything fussy or frivolous. This is for those who are willing to splurge for air-conditioned dining splendor and mix fine food with good conversation and romance.

You'll want to get dressed up—jackets for men (still no tie), and ladies in their finest resort wear.

The *à la carte* menu is Continental cuisine presented with European flair. The service is impeccable.

Snails, artichoke salad, or lobster soup are great ways to begin. Broiled lobster and breast of duck with mango and black pepper sauce are house specialties. Trout amandine, lobster thermidor, and pepper steak are a few of the most popular dishes. If your taste buds long for a juicy Chateaubriand, that's here, too.

Charlotte Russe, almond parfait, and Sou Grand Marnier souffle are among the tempting desserts. After that, you're on your own.

Maxmilian's is open from 7 P.M. to midnight every day. Dinner for two costs about $20–$35 U.S. per person, including local wine. Call 5–80–50 for reservations.

If you want to eat authentic French cuisine in the tropics as Acapulco residents and visitors have been doing for more than 18 years, you'll find your way to **Normandie.**

Everybody agrees that if there is any good French food in town, it's here. The tiny place is run by a French lady, Madame Chauvin, and her daughter.

It's right on the mountain side of the Costera on the corner of Malaespina Street beside El Sol de Acapulco. There is no view, but air conditioning makes up for that. Those who prefer to eat outdoors can do so. Specify your preference when you reserve. The decor is sensible, European tropical. Little money was spent on making this place plush. Soft blue walls, cream-colored furniture, a tiny fountain, and classical music give it Old World appeal.

The clientele is an age mix of diners who like French cuisine. One doesn't come here to be seen. The cuisine, not the scene, is what counts.

The food is delicious. Meals are prepared to order, and chefs are supervised by Madame or her daughter. Dinner for two with local wine is $20–$30 U.S.

Normandie is open daily from 6 P.M. to midnight. It's closed from June to November. Telephone 5–19–16 or 5–13–35 for reservations.

Coyuca 22 on 22 Avenida Coyuca in Old Acapulco is a special place. It is rather like dining in the garden of an elegant old California home. The clientele is made up of discriminating Americans, Canadians, and Europeans. Lobster and prime rib are specialties. After dinner, you can have coffee under the stars while you sit by the pool.

This is not the place to go if you're in a loud party mood. Coyuca 22 is for those who like fine dining in a refined atmosphere, and for those who don't mind paying high prices. This is one of the, if not *the,* most expensive restaurants in town. Dinner can cost $50–$55 U.S. per person.

Coyuca 22 is one of a very few restaurants that isn't open all year round. It's open from Nov. 1 through April

30, daily, from 7 P.M. to midnight. For reservations, call 2–34–68 or 3–50–30.

Regina's Restaurant, upstairs in Plaza Icacos, is air-conditioned and has an elegant air. Waiters wear black tie, and soft music plays in the background. It's too new to tell how the food will be when it is in full operation. Chateaubriand, pepper steak, and other tempting fish and chicken dishes are featured. Open for dinner only, 7 P.M.–midnight. Phone: 4–86–53.

Brand new **El Campanario** (Bell Tower) looks like an Italian castle perched on top of a hill overlooking everything. It's big (capacity 800), beautiful, multi-leveled, and has a marvelous staircase. It's worth 1,000 pesos taxi fare just to have a drink at the bar and walk around to look at the panoramic views.

Continental cuisine takes a long time to get to the table and sometimes arrives cold. However, that doesn't mean that you might not luck out and get a hot tasty meal with hearty portions of meat, chicken, or fish. The price, $20–$25 U.S. per person with domestic wine, is surprisingly low for this opulent place. The owner has a good thing going if he can improve on the food and service. Few places in town are this pretty.

Call 4–88–30 for reservations.

POPULAR HANGOUTS

These places don't have a view of the bay, but that doesn't affect their popularity one bit. You're likely to find a favorite among them and go back night after night. And you'll probably run into someone you know from back home.

Dinners in these places are a little bit more substantial than in most other places in town. You're also likely to have more courses, and the bill might be one or two dollars more per person than in a seaside restaurant. The average starting price for dinner with local wine or beer is approximately $10–$12 U.S. per person.

Kycho's is a popular, informal spot that both residents and visitors like for light meals. It's a place to see and be seen, especially at dinner. On Wednesday nights, the place goes crazy with backgammon tournaments and funny *loteria* (Mexican bingo) games where you buy a card and play by picture. Very amusing. You can hustle up other backgammon tournaments at just about any hour. Kycho's is open 2:00 P.M.–2:00 A.M. every day but Sunday. Tel: 4–07–05.

No one could say that the décor of **El Embarcadero** isn't different. A few steps off the Costera across from Suntory and you feel as if you're in Polynesia. The entrance to this exotic place looks like a Far-Eastern jungle. When you get past the ponds, through the thick foliage (don't worry, there's a walkway) and the screaming birds and monkeys, you'll end up in a replica of a jungle trading post.

They're not kidding: This *is* like Polynesia. The menu is exotic. Malaysian shrimp, Tahitian tempura, chicken Rangoon, Bangkok filet tidbits and Kona steak all have plenty of Far-Eastern flavor.

Those with less exotic tastes can sink their teeth into more familiar fare like T-bone steaks, prime ribs, or surf and turf with stuffed baked potatoes.

El Embarcadero is on the Costera west of the Hyatt Regency. You'll find mostly tourists here from 6 P.M. to 1 A.M. everyday. For reservations, telephone 4–87–87 or 4–27–20.

The new **Spaghetti Factory** across from El Embarcadero is daring and different. You can order tantalizing plates of pasta from a long, appetizing list. Informality reigns. This is new and looks like a winner.

D'Joint is a small place beside the sea. The atmosphere is slightly claustrophobic and there's no view of the ocean, but that doesn't affect its popularity. Locals particularly like it. The food does the trick. Hefty portions of roast beef, charcoal rib-eye steaks, big baked potatoes, and a sumptuous soup-and-salad bar head the menu. All of it is served upstairs.

Downstairs, there are a few tables and a barefoot bar, cable TV, and a game room where you can order up pies and sandwiches.

The booze list makes good reading. Take a look even if you're a teetotaler.

D'Joint is on the Costera near the Holiday Inn. It's open nightly from 7 P.M. to midnight. Phone 4–87–80 for reservations.

At **Su Casa** you get double your money's worth. You not only get good, moderately priced meals for breakfast and lunch, but you also get a spectacular view of the bay from high above the Convention Center. This restaurant is higher up than any others, in a quiet residential section. It's easy to spot at night. Just look for the big lighted arches on the hill.

A sign on the Costera just past the Convention Center leads you up a steep, winding road to Avenida Anahuac. Come up here in a taxi unless you're an expert at parking. If you brave it, leave your car with the attendant, who knows how to weasel around on a precipice.

Climbing the steps up to the front door is guaranteed to work up an appetite.

Once you're up there, you'll find that the owners, a popular local Mexican and his attractive American wife, are not kidding. This *is* their casa, and you're sitting on a very pretty patio just below their front porch with an unobstructed view of the bay.

The menu is simple, but there's something for everybody. Appetizers are especially good. The rose of tomato vinaigrette and the ceviche are both winners. Follow them with the meat or shrimp dishes and you'll be more than satisfied. You'll probably find the whole place so cozy and relaxing that you'll want to linger over coffee. This is a no-nonsense place that delivers value in an open-air dining room.

Those who want to can enjoy pre-dinner or after-dinner drinks in the air-conditioned bar just below.

La Margarita, their brand new sister restaurant, is just "downstairs." The tiled entrance way and the Mexican colonial décor are pretty enough to use as locations for fashion photographs. This, too, has the look and feel of a gracious colonial Mexican home.

The menu offers the kind of Mexican food that you've come to love: guacamole, chile con carne, tacos, enchiladas, chile rellenos, etc., which can be ordered separately or as part of combination plates. Meat and fish dishes and special salads and desserts are also available. Margaritas, a specialty of the house, come by the pitcher and start your meal off with a bang.

Su Casa is open for lunch and dinner from 12:30 P.M. to 12:30 A.M.; La Margarita, dinner only from 6:00 P.M. to midnight. The reservations numbers are 4–30–50 or 4–12–61.

The décor of **Hard Times** is true to that era, but the food certainly isn't. It's plentiful and beautifully displayed. Produce spills out of attractive bamboo boxes, portraying the impression of plenty. Hard Times has some of the best steaks in town, and also serves barbecued ribs, fresh lobster, and shrimp.

Decorations are crazy but pleasant. New Yorkers will feel right at home because street signs with familiar New York street names greet you. Palm trees grow up through the outdoor dining room floor. Some table tops are made from laminated comic strips. The bar is air-conditioned. Meals might include potato skins stuffed with guacamole, steak, stuffed shrimp, or a make-your-own-taco plate.

Professionalism shows here. These are Carlos 'n Charlie's graduates in food as well as gimmicks, and all goes as smooth as clockwork. The clientele is mostly English-speaking.

The restaurant is open for dinner every night from 6:00 P.M. to 12:30 A.M. You can find it upstairs at 400 Costera M. Aleman, across from the Holiday Inn. The sign is hard to see. Look for the red neon lights over the narrow street entrance awning. Call 4–00–64 for reservations.

You dine under the stars at **Chez Guillaume,** overlooking the Costera on the corner of Avenida del Prado, across from the Torre de Acapulco. The actual address is No. 110 Avenida del Prado, about half a block straight up the hill.

This place has reached the status of an Acapulco tradition, and is a long-standing favorite with repeat visitors. You'll find clientele of all ages and nationalities, a sophisticated atmosphere, and surprisingly comfortable outdoor dining. Those who like air-conditioning can find it at the bar.

The menu ranges from French to Continental and American food. Caviar, escargots Chambertin, duck à l'orange, and chicken Kiev are menu items you won't find in very many Acapulco restaurants. The desserts will make you break your diet. Will it be crepes Suzette, baked Alaska, or the mouth-watering Grand Marnier or chocolate soufflé? If it's the latter, order when you order your entrée so you won't have to wait.

Chez Guillaume is open Monday through Saturday from 6:30 P.M. to 12:30 A.M. The reservations numbers are 4–12–31 and 4–12–32. They answer from 9 A.M. on.

There are lots of good reasons to dine at **Pepe & Co.** If there is a tropical "21 Club," this is it. It's an informal restaurant that everybody likes—and everybody likes Pepe, too. If there were a popularity contest for restaurateurs on the Costera, Pepe Valle would win first prize, hands down. His welcome is warm and his hospitality is genuine. Even in season, when just about any food served anywhere will be gobbled up without complaint, Pepe makes an effort to serve high quality, good-value meals, and he honestly cares whether you like them or not.

Pepe's is upstairs right beside Carlos 'n Charlie's on the Costera, but doesn't pretend to be anything like it. The atmosphere here is that of an open-air club where everybody seems to know everybody else, even if they don't. It's warm, friendly, unhurried, and far less frantic and flip than next door.

The menu is Continental and prices are moderate. No matter how many times you come back you'll always find something that you like to eat. Pepe's minestrone soup just might be the best in the world. The steak and broiled lobster are delicious, and so is just about anything else on the menu.

Before and after dinner, or maybe both, you can slip into the attractive air-conditioned piano bar where Chacon's piano tunes keep everyone on the verge of singing along.

Pepe's crowd is a mix of residents, tourists, Americans, Mexicans, Europeans, and Canadians: families, pre-disco diners, after-theater snackers, and those who just plain like easy, sensible, good value meals in a more than pleasant open-air atmosphere.

The sign outside reads: "One cannot think well, live well, or love well if one has not dined well"—at Pepe's, of course! And that's just about true.

Pepe's is open every day for lunch (except Sunday) and dinner from 1:00 P.M. to midnight. The reservation numbers are 4–70–88 and 4–70–89.

Carlos 'n Charlie's lights up the Costera in more ways than one. Everyone—but everyone—who comes to Acapulco, regardless of age, income, or social status, seems to cross its portals at least once. Its popularity has been overwhelming since the day the doors opened, and its fame has spread throughout the world.

It's a crowd pleaser that packs 'em in upstairs across from the Condesa del Mar every night except Tuesdays, when the waiters get a day off to unwind and "go fishing" —and most of them need it. They're natural-born joksters who are as good as stand-up comedians. Flip and flirty waiters, joke menus, and good food are trademarks of the successful Carlos Anderson chain. Just reading the menu will give you some chuckles. These are the originators of the Oink, Moo, Cluck, and Splash menus, and that gives you a clue as to what to expect when you order. But don't worry, the food is serious, plentiful, and good value.

The humor and the food have universal appeal. The dress runs the gamut from bluejeans to mink, and the clientele from grandee to baby sister.

There are no reservations. You just have to wait your turn. Early diners begin to form lines outside the door just after 6:00 P.M. The door opens at 6:30 and the line is always long and lasts until late. But then, standing in line is a great way to meet people.

The big air-conditioned bar is another good meeting place. What it lacks in esthetics is compensated for by numbers. Singles with wandering eyes congregate here, along with residents and everyone else.

Almost any table is good. The crowds know what they're waiting for and they like it.

Hours are 6:30 P.M. to midnight. You'll probably see

the wound-up waiters after 2:00 A.M. at the disco. If you're lucky, maybe they'll invite you to come along.

One thing is for *sure* about this place: You'll *never* be bored.

Pepe's Las Tablitas (no relation to Pepe & Co.) is one of a kind. There are lots of other streetside snack stands, but this one at No. 200 Costera M. Aleman, across from the big gray Nacional Financiera building down from the Acapulco Plaza ranks way above the rest.

You can drop in just about any time from noon until midnight in your bathing suit or your ballgown (though the latter would probably cause a disturbance), and have a wonderfully big meal for a wonderfully small amount of money.

This is a place where looks are deceiving. The similarity between it and the host of other sidewalk places stops with the sidewalk.

Pepe is a graduate of Las Brisas, where he learned how to serve up clean and tasty food that everyone likes. Wooden tables on a streetside concrete floor and a couple of old bullfight posters are just about the only décor. He doesn't waste money on fine china and crystal, either.

But the good food and the good prices compensate for the lack of esthetics. Pepe's spareribs with Chimichurri are among the world's most mouthwatering treats.

A lunch or dinner that will fill you up for a day can cost less than $5 U.S. No credit cards here, it's strictly pay as you eat. The restaurant is open from 12:00 noon to 12:00 midnight. Pepe's is one of the biggest bargains in town. A tip: Try to sit as far away from the outdoor grill as you can. No reservations.

La Fogata de Charly, a tiny, hole-in-the-wall jewel of a place between the Acapulco Plaza and the Maralisa Hotels, is another "find" where you can have a tasty, hearty meal of lobster or meat for under $5 and get a live folklore show thrown in free of charge. It is a miniscule family trattoria that recalls the Good Old Days. This kind of friendly family place is a dying breed. It is one of the few places where you can join Mexican tourists, enjoy the true traditional flavor of Old Acapulco, and see the shows that led to today's glitz. Being tiny makes it hard to find, but it's worth the search. La Fogata de Charly is open for lunch and dinner. Check the *comida corrida* for lunch. The price (about $2 U.S.) is right.

SEASIDE

Acapulco seaside restaurants are sunsational. Where else in the world can you dance barefoot in your bikini if you dare, or take a dip in the ocean between courses if you're in the mood? There are no other dining places as carefree as these on a bright, sunny day.

Fun and surprises are there for the taking. You can shop, eat, dance, and swim from your table if you want to. You can have your photo taken kissing a chimp, have your caricature drawn, buy a serape, a T-shirt, or a record. Your meal can be as crazy or as quiet as you want it to be. You might be given a flower shower. You might do a sassy samba with a waiter. Or you might order up a cocoloco with two straws, linger over a seafood entrée, listen to the music and the waves, and share a dream or two.

Get used to the presence of strolling photographers, even at lunch. They're following up on the Mexican idea that every restaurant and disco visit is a celebration that you'll want to remember.

The handful of restaurants overlooking the ocean between the Condesa del Mar and the Hyatt Continental probably don't count the number of people that they feed and entertain every year, but if they did the number would probably add up to millions whose homes are scattered all over the globe.

What makes them so outstanding is their informality and spontaneity. They're places where you can let it all hang out if you want to, or places that are as romantic as can be if you're in a loving mood. They're places that let you make whatever you want to out of a meal. Anything from pure "pachanga" (party plus) to a tête-à-tête goes.

Those that are open for both lunch and dinner, like Beto's and Paradise, have different personalities by day and by night. Most are party places where delicious lobster, shrimp, and seafood are served up with plenty of lively music and fun. They open around 11:00 A.M. and stay open until 11:30 or midnight. The sound of the waves is spelled by the sound of the music, and the passing parade of vendors on the beach never leaves you with a dull moment. As a matter of fact, you could do all of your shopping from a ringside seat next to the railing overlooking the beach at some restaurants. But once the word gets around to the itinerant vendors that you're buying, you'd better be prepared not to take more than two bites without interruption from yet another souvenir seller.

Don't pay attention to the noisy little boys who sometimes come along with the vendors. Those kids yell instead of sing and then expect to be tipped for it. They're relentless and will keep up the racket all afternoon for a few pesos if encouraged.

Some of the restaurants also serve under *palapas* (thatched lean-tos) on the sand, but unless you're ready to run when the tide comes in or have a friend who will chase the precocious flies, you should eat in the restaurants a few steps away. The meal price is the same, but the scene gives you triple your money's worth. Beto's and Paradise are two of the most popular beach and dining-room operations.

By day, Mexicans and foreign visitors together account for the overwhelming popularity of the seaside places. By night, there is a visible change in the clientele, and foreign accents predominate.

Nights are particularly romantic. Silhouettes of palm trees, murmuring waves, and moonlight on the water set the mood.

In general, seafood is the specialty, and the free-wheeling fun comes right along with it. Almost all restaurants accept major credit cards.

Most don't take reservations for one or two, but call ahead if you have a big group. Lunch or dinner in any of these places will cost $10–$15 U.S. per person, including local wine or beer and depending on how much you eat. Lunch is the main meal of the day.

You won't find anything like the Acapulco seaside restaurants anywhere else in the world. Everybody should try one. Dining in these fun-filled places by the sea can be like watching a movie.

Safari Bar & Restaurant, heading the pack on the Costera, has so much Polynesian atmosphere that you have to remind yourself that you're still in North America. The bar is pure Bogart. The restaurant is hidden away downstairs, where you dine under the stars overlooking the ocean. Try to get a table by the railing. The fare is fair and medium priced, but the ambience is strictly Far Eastern romance. Open for dinner only, from 6 to midnight. No phone, ergo no reservations.

Beto's is the five-star darling of the beach-side restaurants. Its food is a few notches above the others, and somehow it manages to create a slight air of dignity, though most of the lunchtime diners arrive in bathing suits and coverups.

Most days, there is lively live music for those who want to dance. If you'd rather talk than listen, sit in the section on the left at the bottom of the steps.

The food has gotten rave notices since 1950. The menu offers a wider variety of choices than most other beachside places. The chefs also make mouthwatering dishes that aren't on the list. Those in the know know about Beto's branch in the tiny village of Barra Vieja where the *pièce de résistance* is an Acapulco specialty called "Pescado a la Talla." It's a split, grilled snapper with a sauce that tastes slightly barbecue flavored. Ask—you have nothing to lose. If they have this dish at Beto's on the Costera, forget everything else and try it. The same goes for *Quesadillas de Cazon,* tortillas filled with baby shark meat and fried. There's a special art to making both of these dishes just right, and Beto knows how to do it.

Split the quesadillas with a loved one unless you have a big appetite, or are willing to miss the main course.

They're open every day from 10:00 A.M. to 12:00 midnight. The locals start trickling in around 2:30 P.M.. Call 4–04–73 for reservations.

Barbas Negras—Blackbeard's—looks as if a pirate just went out the door. It's got he-man sized tables, a he-man sized salad bar, and he-man sized helpings of lobster thermidor, shrimp, and steaks.

The salty rum-runners atmosphere has been a big success. Blackbeard's was one of the first seaside restaurants, and is still going strong.

Some tables overlook the ocean, some don't. There are no reservations, but a table with a view is worth waiting for. It's open daily from 6:00 P.M. to 12 P.M.

Watch out, ladies, this place has surprises in the john!

Mimi's Chili Saloon is a gas. It has just about all of the familiar food that you may be missing, plus some.

The signs are the best on the Costera. The promise of giant mango or peach margaritas, two for one at Happy Hour, make you want to step right up to this powder-blue palace. In this case, it's down.

The bar is for those with foot fetishes. The only view is of feet and ankles walking along the Costera.

If you go to Happy Hour, be sure to take a friend. Someone will have to carry you home if you have two of those delicious frozen margaritas.

The rest of the restaurant has a view of the ocean on two levels. The menu is packed with back-home favorites. All-American hamburgers (the best in town), onion rings, home fries, potato skins, country-fried chicken, fried fresh mushrooms, and hot dogs are all designed to make you drool.

Mimi's is right next to Blackbeard's. It's open daily from 6:00 P.M. to midnight. You can't miss it; a young crowd hangs out here.

You walk down the red steps to **Paradise** at the sign of the Red Fish. Downstairs, it's loco, delightful pandemonium. Paradise is still reigning queen of the seaside restaurants. This was one of the first party restaurants on the beach. And the party hasn't stopped since it opened. Anyone who likes to get the fun rolling early can find it here. So kick off your shoes, grab a piña colada, and you're on your way to good times.

Most people arrive revved up and ready to go in bathing suits with coverups. Some women don't bother much about the coverups. Live salsa music begins around 2:00 P.M. The rhythm is contagious and you can dance in nothing more than a bikini if you dare. This is a place where almost anything goes.

The fun gets crazier as the afternoon goes on. Heaven help you if the word gets out that it's your birthday or anniversary. You might be picked up on your chair, set on a table, get a beautiful girl dumped in your lap (vice versa if you're a girl) and be showered with flower petals while the waiters sing the Mexican version of Happy Birthday, "Mananitas."

The clientele is a little bit of anywhere. The waiters are pranksters with aprons. The fun begins at the bottom of the steps when some of the staff sneak up and drop a lei over each lady's head. Everything stops when a pretty girl walks in. The waiters gather round and shout "aloha" and everyone who wants to gets into the act.

Just down from Mimi's Chili Saloon, **Paradise** is open for lunch and dinner. Lunch is when most of the big-time shenanigans take place. Dinner is a bit quieter, but whichever you choose the fun will be there. And so, probably, will be the trained monkey who is pretty good at pranks herself. She loves to give you a big smooch for the cameras and has been accused of working in cahoots with the house photographer.

One meal here, and you don't have to eat for the rest of the day. The menu is simple and delicious. Drinks and portions are man-sized. It's either shrimp, lobster, or steak—and it's all good and fresh.

They also serve under palapas on the beach, where you can rent a chair. If you plan to make a day of it, get there early, at around 11:30, and get a second-or third-row (from the water's edge) palapa. You won't want to move when the waves come in!

Paradise is open at 12:00 noon–12:00 midnight every day. $10–$15 U.S. will get you about all you can eat. Paradise is open noon through midnight. Prime time for lunch is between 2:00 and 4:00 P.M. Tel.: 4–59–88. No reservations.

Barbarroja, across from Hotel Fiesta Tortuga, is one of the newest kids on the "block" of seaside places. This one has a pirate motif and a wide-open feeling. It should. The roof over your head is the sky and there are no walls, only a low railing.

Don't dine here if you don't want to be seen. Tables with red-and-white checked cloths are one step up from the sidewalk and the only thing to obstruct passerby's view of you and your meal is a giant ship's mast. The good news is that your view of the bay is virtually unobstructed, too.

Even the menu is out on the sidewalk for all to see. It caters to gringo appetites for traditional dining-out dishes like shrimp, steak, lobster tails, and surf'n turf. An air-conditioned piano bar will help you work up an appetite or enjoy the fat-cat after-dinner feeling. After-dinner drinks are on the house.

Barbarroja is open from 6:30 P.M. to 12:30 A.M. every night. No reservations.

It's easy to get the wrong idea about the **Crazy Lobster (Langosta Loca).** They put grungy food (sometimes plastic, sometimes real) wrapped in saran wrap on the wall outside to attract customers strolling along the Costera. Unfortunately, the display couldn't be more unappetizing. It only makes you want to shut your eyes and walk past quickly.

However, those willing to risk it are in for a big treat. As your meal progresses, you discover that the Crazy Lobster isn't so crazy after all. In fact, it is one of the most sophisticated and dignified of the beachside restaurants on The Strip. Service is excellent. Some dishes are prepared to order at the table, just as they would be in the finest restaurant.

The décor is beige stucco, like Baby O's. Tables and chairs are attractive light wood and straw. Two fish tanks that have lots more than lobster—and not all of it is meant to end up on a plate—are the focal points.

Lobster, snapper (*hauchinango*), and other specialties are delicious. The open-air patio by the sea is pleasant and comfortable. If you don't want your conversation interrupted after every sentence by flocks of vendors offering a "surprise" if you'll give them your name (the surprise is a small hand-painted picture with your name on it that will cost you 500 pesos), sit on the left side of the restaurant. That's the part that is too high for the vendors to reach. The Crazy Lobster is open for lunch and dinner from 10:00 A.M. to 11:30 P.M. Tel: 4–59–74.

THE ELITE MEET

The **Villa Vera Hotel and Racquet Club Restaurant** has always been a favorite with the fun-loving jet set and with discriminating international visitors.

It's strictly a class act. It feels like a private club, and looks like a page out of *Town & Country* on any day of the week. The people-watching is supreme.

The open-air restaurant has three beautiful views: the bar and pool area, the bay, and the people.

Lunches are to be lingered over. European-trained chefs innovate delicious dishes and scrumptious desserts. Fish Orly with a curry dip, sea bass in white wine sauce, and chateaubriand are among the favorite dishes. Fresh apple, banana, and pineapple fritters with ice cream are the most popular dessert.

At lunchtime (12:00 noon to 4:00 P.M.) the atmosphere is just what it promises—that of a beach club with a view complete with pool splashing. At night, things quiet down and become deliciously romantic. A piano bar with soft music adds another nice touch.

This is one of the prettiest, most popular, most sophisticated restaurants in town. Any international celebrity who can slip away from his host and hostess is likely to show up here.

The Villa Vera Restaurant is open every day from noon to midnight. Call 4–03–33. Lunch costs approximately $10–$15 U.S. per person. Dinner is about $20–$30 U.S. including local wine.

MEXICAN MUNCHIES

Uppity residents will tell you that there's no really good Mexican food in Acapulco. Wrong! Good Mexican dishes can be found all over town. You only have to choose the degree of formality you'd like to dine in.

Los Rancheros, up on the Scenic Highway just

before you reach Las Brisas, is open for lunch as well as dinner. This is an informal al fresco place that is a favorite with locals, Mexican tourists, and visitors of all nationalities who are in-the-know. Everybody loves a bargain and this can be it! However, if you're a habitue, be prepared. New management has made the portions much smaller and the food quality varies from meal to meal. But, the million-dollar view and budget prices make it worth the trip. If you don't want to risk a disappointing dinner, just come for drinks.

This is one of the few restaurants that serve Bohemia, one of the zestiest of Mexican beers. When the chef is "on," Chicken Enchiladas with Green Sauce and Queso Fundido are a good bet.

You won't find the jet set up here. They pay double for the same view just up the hill at Madeiras and Miramar. To get double your money's worth, go for a late lunch or an early dinner and watch the sun set and the lights begin to sparkle along Acapulco Bay.

Two can dine for under $20 U. S. and the view is worth a billion. Los Rancheros is open from 1 P.M. to midnight. Call 4–19–08 for reservations.

Cocula's are dotted around town. These Mexican steak houses are just about as informal as Mexican restaurants can get. There's one outdoors in El Patio Shopping Center that's open from 6:00 P.M. until midnight, but the one near the Exelaris Hyatt Regency seems to be everyone's favorite. Look for the sign of the sombrero. Chicken and beef tacos and spareribs are excellent. So are the tasty sauces. A "secret" room in the back is open to all—it's an air-conditioned bar! Its menu is meat oriented and its tacos are tops. Everybody seems to like it. Wait for a table downstairs. Upstairs fills with smoke from the grill.

Pancho's is a pretty new Mexican restaurant by the sea just below the Crazy Lobster where you can watch your meal of Mexican specialties being prepared in a spic-and-span kitchen. $12–$15 U.S. will get you the most expensive entrée there is.

Los Arcos in the Acapulco Plaza Hotel is the only place where you can eat delicious Mexican food in an elegant, air-conditioned setting. Men can wear shirt and pants, but women will want to dress up a bit.

If you're with a group, order a variety of dishes, as you would a Chinese dinner, and share. The "Make Your Own Tacos" (*Haga Su Taco*) plate is a wonderful way to begin. Melted cheese, chicken, venison, sausage, beans, guacamole, and tortillas come to your table in a big clay dish so you can make whatever taco tempts your tastebuds.

Follow it with broiled beef *tampiquena* garnished with guacamole and refried beans, or *quesadillas* of fish, beef, or mushrooms.

Dulce de papaya (papaya with caramel) coconut custard, and coyote *sonorense,* tortilla with molasses, will more than satisfy your sweet tooth. Finish with *Café de Olla,* a strong Mexican coffee with cinnamon and sugar cooked into it.

Los Arcos is open for dinner only, every night from 7 P.M. to midnight. Call 5-80-50 for reservations.

Diehard connoisseurs of Mexican food with strong stomachs, some knowledge of Spanish, and a taxi driver who is willing to turn detective in order to find the place can go to **Tlaquepaque.** It's as hard to pronounce as it is to find. It's located in the front garden of a house in a residential section just above The Strip. Even residents are confused about its location. But they all seem to take time to find it, especially on Thursdays, which is *pozole* (thick corn soup) day.

The owner doesn't encourage gringo sissies to pass his portals. But he does cater to anyone who really shows enthusiasm for the food. You have to know your Mexican dishes before you come to Tlaquepaque, for the menu isn't translated; but if you do, chances are you'll have a big treat. Tlaquepaque is at Calle Uno, Lote F, in Colonia Vista Alegre. It's open from 1:00 p.m. to midnight every day except Monday. Have your hotel call 5-61-69 or 5-70-55 for reservations. Very little English spoken here.

Nightlife

Nothing in the world matches Acapulco's nightlife. It's as star-spangled, glittering, and kinetic as it comes. You can begin another full "day" of fun *after* the sun goes down. The bay lights up after dark and stays that way until dawn. The fun goes on as long as you can last. The number of alternatives for what you can do with an evening is staggering. Some of the world's most romantic restaurants and dazzling discos are there for you to choose from.

Full-fledged nightclub shows with big-name entertainers take place around town, too. Banneret in the Holiday Inn, Cocoloco at the Princess, and Mil Luces at the Hyatt Regency are just a few of the places where world-class international entertainment is likely to show up. (The price of an equivalent show back home would probably be triple.)

If a Flamenco fling is your trip, go to El Fuerte in front of Las Hamacas Hotel. If salsa turns you on, join the fun at Nina's near CiCi. It's 100% Latin, but everyone is welcome. If you go for male or female strippers, try Chippendale's.

If you're looking for something racy, every taxi driver knows where La Huerta, the Red Light District, is. It's better to go by cab. They'll call one when you're ready to leave. Here, you can have your choice of a grotesque but amusing Afro Casino show where you don't need to understand Spanish to get the jokes. The Dance Hall is next door; you can go with your date or find one who will dance with you for a price. La Huerta is safe as long as you don't flirt with someone else's lady or let someone else flirt with yours. It is *not* the place to bring anyone who wants to be surrounded by the Upper Crust or who will be shocked by juvenile sex shows.

THE DRINKS

Mexican bartenders don't lack imagination. Your drinks might arrive in a whole pineapple decorated with fruit and flowers, or in a coconut. Whatever it is, it will probably have more than one kind of impact.

Mexicans mix tequila, the heady national drink, with just about anything. Tequila "poppers" (Tequila shaken up in a shot glass with 7-Up) are an Acapulco invention served in discotheques with the idea of giving you an instant high. One won't, but two might. Margaritas, tequila sours, or sunrises, *petroleos* (a do-it-yourself mix of tequila, maguey sauce, and lemon juice) are just a few of the other countless popular concoctions. Or, you can take it the way the Mexicans do—straight, with salt and lemon and an occasional beer chaser, or with Sangrita, a mix of tomato juice, orange juice, maguey sauce, and chiles. Whatever you do, proceed with caution. Some tequilas are 90 proof. *Conmemorativo,* slightly more expensive, is for those who like it older and smoother.

Rum is another popular drink. If you're on a budget, stay with this. Imported hard liquors and wines carry premium prices.

Mexican beers are tasty, zesty, and on a par with the world's best. Carta Blanca, Bohemia, and Superior are popular brands. Why Mexicans put salt and lemon on the rim of the Tecate beer can is a mystery. Brisa is the light beer, but it has a metallic aftertaste. Negra Modelo is dark, as is Dos Equìs.

Colas and sodas abound, but the diet craze hasn't hit Mexico yet. If you look hard, you might find Diet Pepsi or Tab, but if you want any other lo-cal drink, B.Y.O.

Most hotels have their own water purification plants. Or you can order bottled mineral water such as Tehuacan with (*con*) or without (*sin*) bubbles (*gas*). Add a bit of lime to make a seaside refresher, and drink everything without ice if you're outside your hotel and in doubt.

THE DAZZLING DISCOS

Discos are open 365 days a year from 10:00 P.M. until the last customer goes home. You can make reservations in most of them if you have a big group. Call between 9:00 A.M. and 1:00 P.M. or 4:00 P.M. and 7:00 P.M. The energy expended on an Acapulco dance floor on any given night could probably generate enough power to light up New York City a few days. Anyone from the ages of 19 to 90 should experience an Acapulco disco at least once in a lifetime.

All have cover charges. They range from $5 to $15 per person, depending on the place. It's usually paid in cash at the door, not on your bill. When the crowds come on long weekends in Mexico City, some discos raise their cover charge, but the price includes all you can drink. Most accept reservations and major credit cards.

If you really want to get your money's worth, go at prime time—11:30 P.M. until 2:00 A.M., especially if you're single. Everyone is usually paired off by 1:00 A.M. This is when the electricity is at its peak. In season, you might have to leave your hotel at 11:00 P.M. to get in by 1:00 A.M. if you want to arrive at the peak of the frenzy, but it's fun to go earlier and watch it build up.

Most often, from December–April, there are big crowds at the door, but waiting is worth it. People will still be going in at 5:30 A.M., but most of the real action is over by then.

Follow your fantasies when dressing. Some people's suitcases might be mistaken for a circus performer's, but you get the idea: *anything* goes as long as it almost covers the parts that ought to be covered. In season, you'll see everything from evening dresses to mini-dresses and cowboy boots. If there has been a costume party somewhere that night (and in Acapulco that's a frequent occurrence) you're liable to find yourself dancing beside an Arab in full regalia, a Chinese, a pirate, or a Carmen Miranda look-alike. Everything and anything goes. That's Acapulco.

The same applies to the rest of the year, when dress is more normal. However, no woman in her right mind would appear in an Acapulco disco looking anything other than her very best. You can go in tropical office clothes if you want to, but this is one time when you should look more dazzling than the place. Looking carefully and tastefully put together and maybe a bit more risqué than you would at home is vital. So wear your best disco outfit or a pretty, cool dress no longer than midcalf length. Men can wear anything *except* socks and ties. A well-cut silk or cotton shirt and pants and loafers are chic, easy, and practical.

Though all of the discos are air conditioned, so much motion means that they're *hot,* so make sure that whatever you wear is light, and not too restricted. From December to March when crowds are thickest women might take a fan or a barette to hold your hair up when the dance floor frenzy peaks.

GETTING IN

This is the million-dollar question.

Getting into one of the leading discos, especially in season, will tax your ingenuity. Crowds at the door can approximate New York's Grand Central Station at rush hour, and can be more rude. Even if you've made reservations you usually have to wait. The basis for admittance is definitely *not* first come, first served.

Disco "doorman" has become a coveted profession in Acapulco. They're the people whom everyone knows or wants to know. They're crowd readers, crowd pushers, and crowd appeasers, whose job it is to admit the people who will make the crowd inside their place look better and livelier.

The girls have the upper hand. If you're with a stunning lady, your chances of instant admittance more than doubles. In general, single men are not admitted until there are enough single ladies inside. So single men should do their sorting out at the beach clubs or around the pool during the day, instead of waiting until the last moment.

However, any couple that stands tall and looks classy and as if they *expect* to be admitted usually is. Just jockey your way within the near vision of the man at the door, catch his eye, smile, stay in one spot and wait like ladies and gentleman. Chances are that you'll be among the first to enter. Don't be discouraged if you're older. That means you have status, rank, and priority! Once you're admitted, tip the doorman 500–1,000 pesos or more if you plan to come back.

Remember, *all* of the discos are electric. If you can't get into Numero Uno, all is not lost. Plenty of action takes place at the others. Numbers 2 and 3 were probably Number One a short time ago.

The delicious chaos begins once you're beyond the velvet cord. Most discos charge an entry fee that ranges from $5 to $15 per person, depending on the place, during December through Easter Week. New Year's Eve is an entity in itself. It's a special occasion which is often handled like a private club where tables are pre-sold.

Once you're in, tip the maitre d' or waiter who gives you a table anywhere from $2 to $3 and up. Look at this tip as a long-term investment for when you come back. Whether or not you plan to come back, tip at least 1,000 pesos if the table is good. After all, this is the man who gives you position. The bigger the tip, the better the table. Regardless of the hour, he'll probably have to rearrange some people to squeeze you in. So get used to rubbing elbows with strangers. Offer the waiter a tip in advance, too: $2 to $3 should guarantee good service on a crowded night.

A bad table only depends on your point of view. Some people love being next to the dance floor or under the speakers. Those who want to chat or communicate by anything other than telepathy should go somewhere else. Locals think that the discos do have a Siberia, but only snobs take that seriously. In most cases, unless you're there to meet and greet, there's not a bad seat in the place. Most of us go to dance and have a good time, and once you're in you'll be doing just that.

Domestic drinks will cost about $2.50–$3.50. White wine and vodka are most popular. Cokes and other nonalcoholic drinks are $1–$1.50. Imported drinks like Scotch (which is called whisky in Mexico, and which you can order by brand name if you like) and bourbon cost about $6. Cognac (domestic) is around $3.50, and imported champagne goes for about $120–$150 a bottle. Depending on the place and the night, tequila poppers might be free. Tip 15 percent of the bill; 20 percent if the service has been good.

Now, let's take the discos as they come.

THE SUPER EIGHT

All but one of the Super Eight discos are on the Strip. Fantasy is the only major disco which is not.

Fantasy, at La Vista, the newest kid on the disco block, is a heady cocktail of panoramic views, old time Acapulco gimmicks, ultramodern videos and laser lights, and world class comfort and elegance.

It grew seemingly overnight into a sophisticated lady whose charm means nights to remember and glittering fun in a spectacular setting. There's nothing like it anywhere in the world!

Fantasy is built on the hill overlooking the bay. The dance area has floor-to-ceiling windows with spectacular views. Only 300 lucky people fit in. The entrance and foyer are your first clues that this place is a cut above the rest. Pretty girls and guys in tuxedos welcome you and take you to your table. Booths are ultra soft and comfortable. Occasional fireworks spill from the roof like all-encompassing waterfalls of stars that light up the night even more. The latest in laser lights illuminate the dance floor. A glass elevator takes you to the second floor, where you can shop for sexy lingerie or Cartier "Le Must" items.

This is a snazzy hangout for the older (25 and up) Las Brisas crowd and for anyone who likes to feel like a millionaire in opulent surroundings. Dress well and arrive between 11:00 P.M. and midnight if you're not a member or not known. This is and looks like the most expensive disco in town. There is an annual membership fee and a card for those who come to Acapulco often; ask about these at the desk. The telephone number is 4–67–27.

Baby O is not only first in line, it's first on the disco hit parade on The Strip.

This is the undisputed Numero Uno on the Strip at the moment, the current reigning Queen in a town where subjects are discriminating and fickle and where you really have to kick higher than anyone else to make the first row. The fact that Baby O has out-gimmicked, out-populated and, for the moment, outdone her competitors is no accident. It's creative thinking, hard work, and a lot of luck.

Baby O has reigned for about five years. It heads the razzle dazzle on the Costera on the corner of Horacio Nelson across from the Romano Palace Hotel toward the Hyatt Regency end of The Costera. Once you've fought your way in, you'll see why it's first. The electricity in the air and the action on the dance floor are overwhelming.

This seven-year-old Baby is a favorite hangout of all age groups. Eighteen to 30 would probably be the average ages on any given night, but weights tip to the lower end of the scale. Big spenders and those who would like to be young come here, too. In short, you're likely to be seeing the "in crowd" from Mexico City and from around the world.

The trouble is that only 500 of them can fit in, and thousands *want* to get in. Furthermore, there always has to be space to pack in any celebrity, jet setter, or millionaire who comes to town, too. You'll still see people arriving at 5:00 A.M. This is a classic example of a seller's market.

Once you've made it inside, you have to be as surefooted as a mountain goat. Stairs to the uneven tiers of tables which surround the dance floor are steep and narrow. You either wear flats or risk a major dental job. There are also tables on tiers still higher on the left side of the dance floor. Mexicans seem to prefer sitting on the bottom level, where part of your view may be nothing more than dancers' feet and ankles. Two other favorite tables are in "caves" at the left and right of the dance floor. The best view is from the tables on the second and third center tiers—just like the theater. What you'll be seeing on any night in the year is a spectacular show and a half—and you'll be among the performers. Most disco devotees will hit Fantasy and Baby O during the night.

A sign outside occasionally claims that they'll age you in a few hours, and that's not far from wrong. The beat is deafening and contagious. Video screens drop from the ceiling periodically. They also have the best T-shirts of all discos in several styles. You can buy them at the door. There is a downstairs snack bar that looks like a Western saloon, where you can refuel your engine with an omelet or a hamburger. The reservations number is 4–74–74. Credit cards are accepted. The entrance fee is about $10 per person.

Magic *is* magic! It's the baby of the Super Six and has the young look of the electronic generation with an older crowd. You'll find the ritzy 18-to-25 crowd here, along with a sprinkle of youngsters.

The décor is different from any other. You realize it before you even get inside. The entrance is a huge open area with an ultramodern look. What other disco has shown you a big fountain, a lily pond, and a house alligator named Antonio before you even go through the front door?

The front door is like the false bottom of a magician's box. It leads up to one of the spacious bars where singles can sit and overlook the dance floor.

The room is large and open, with brass railings and

tiered tables. Booths in the back center promise a conversation or two.

Laser lights and electronic boards where space ships flash light up the night. The music here is a few decibels higher than it is in other discos. If you feel your table vibrating it's not an earthquake; it's just the bass. If you want to talk and overlook the whole scene, grab a table on the level above the T-shirt stand. In some people's opinions the tables here are among the best in the house.

Magic is open seven days a week from 10:00 P.M. until 5:00 A.M. The telephone number is 4-88-15.

Bocaccio is . . . well . . . Bocaccio. It's streamers, champagne, action at the bar, bright lights, and great music, on the Costera, midway down The Strip. It has, perhaps, one of the most faithful followings of all the discos in town. Mexicans and Americans and a big crowd of Canadians who like to party have been flocking here to let go for more than a dozen years. If you look at the New Year's Eve photos from days gone by you'll probably see a lot of the same faces that are there today, and the marvelous good times are still rolling.

Though it has been jazzed up with a sparkling new decor, laser beams, video screens, and electronic boards that can be programmed with surprise personal messages, this place has preserved some of the popular party gimmicks that got Acapulco going. Confetti, balloons, ethnic hour, champagne, and belly-dancing contests at 2:00 A.M. are a few of the old attractions that newcomers and old timers love. Most of the clientele here are a little older—25 to 50 maybe—but a young singles crowd populates three bars clustered together, and it's a good place for singles over 25 to meet someone.

Unlike most other discos, they close the door at 4:00 A.M. whether or not the last clients are ready to leave.

Call 4-19-00 or 4-19-81 for reservations. All credit cards are accepted.

Eve, formerly called UBQ, has had its ups and downs. Right now, under new ownership, it's on an upswing.

Located a short distance from Jackie O, just east of the Diana traffic circle next to Teddy's Beach Club, it still attracts a beautiful international crowd that was faithful to it in its heyday. The Europeans always liked this one in particular, and the signs for a comeback are promising.

It deserves to be back in the ranks of the Big Timers. At this moment in history, it's the only disco located on the ocean. If the doors behind the dance floor suddenly part, you can dance under the stars, hear the delicious sound of the waves above the music, and have a panoramic view of the bay.

There is a comfortable Y-shaped bar. If you want a change of pace you can attack the video games in the room beside it. Tel: 4-47-78.

Jackie O is conveniently located on the corner sandwiched between Midnight and El Patio Shopping Center, and has always been a star. Before the Jackie O poster was attached to the wall it was Charlie's Chili, a spot that was popular with local cops as well as the fast-lane international set. Today, about 80 percent of the clients are Americans, and it also pulls a lot of locals as well as a sprinkling of Europeans in the 25–40 age group. The "action" is good, too, as single women who look elegant are allowed to occupy tables if they don't want to sit at the bar. Tel: 4-87-33.

P.S. The O at the end does not mean that Jackie O and Baby O are related. It's purely coincidental.

Midnight sparkles like no other. Everything about it looks brand new. The décor is shining black and silver. Women love it because whatever they wear stands out. Plush booths line the walls, glossy lacquered mirrors provide glittering light, and you can now walk all the way around the dance floor.

Everyone makes a spectacular entrance. You feel like a movie star arriving at a premiere as you pass through the tunnel that leads in from the door. It lights up as you move along.

Plush banquettes make watching the scene comfortable. You can walk around the dance floor with ease even on a crowded night. Video screens light up the dance floor. There seems to be a constant schedule of special parties. On weekends, they continue during the day as the crowd moves to a beach club out on Revolcadero. To reserve a table, call 4-82-95.

Cats, a few doors down from Midnight, is another

winner. It slipped onto the scene while no one was looking and may be one of the prettiest discos along the Strip.

It evokes a feeling of plushness, comfort and space. Towering "trees" lighted with tiny sparkling lights, tiered chairs and tables, video screens, and a dance floor that is just the right size, combine to make a magical setting. This is an ideal disco to know about if you're looking for a good mix of the latest disco technology and the Acapulco disco mania. Tel: 4–72–35.

INDEX

Index

FODOR'S TRAVEL GUIDES

Here is a complete list of Fodor's Travel Guides, available in current editions; most are also available in a British edition published by Hodder & Stoughton.